"An imaginative way to introduce : _____ dom of C. S. Lewis."

NANCY PEARCEY, AUTHOR OF *TOTAL TRUTH*

"There are few scholars who understand C. S. Lewis's apologetic work as deeply as Art Lindsley. I've known Art for many years and have always been impressed not only by his grasp of Lewis but also by his ability to apply the material in fresh ways. I enjoyed reading *C. S. Lewis's Case for Christ;* it is creatively written and makes Lewis's apologetics accessible to an even wider audience."

JERRY ROOT, PH.D., COEDITOR OF *THE QUOTABLE LEWIS*

"Art Lindsley rightly notes that though we think we see clearly, 'more often we miss certain clues or fail to see the implications of the ones we are given.' So he offers his readers an invaluable map to our confused world through the clear spyglass of C. S. Lewis. In this wonderful examination of the man and his writings, Lindsley points out the obstacles to Lewis's faith in God (obstacles that I often hear from the seeker and skeptic) as well as the ways that Lewis carefully worked through them in his mind and in his heart. I heartily recommend this book."

RAVI ZACHARIAS, AUTHOR AND SPEAKER

"In this excellent book, Art Lindsley presents the vast sweep of C. S. Lewis's worldview in clear, bite-sized pieces. It will be enjoyed by those who are new to Lewis as well as those who have read his work for years, by thoughtful skeptics and by all who share Lewis's 'mere Christianity.' "

CHUCK COLSON, FOUNDER AND CHAIRMAN, PRISON FELLOWSHIP

"The brilliant diamond of Lewis's case for Christ has many facets. Lindsley looks at each in turn, helping first-time Lewis readers see the singular shaft of divine light that each facet reflects."

JAMES SIRE, AUTHOR OF *THE UNIVERSE NEXT DOOR*

C. S. LEWIS'S
CASE FOR
CHRIST

Insights from Reason, Imagination and Faith

ART LINDSLEY

InterVarsity Press
Downers Grove, Illinois

InterVarsity Press
P.O. Box 1400, Downers Grove, IL 60515-1426
World Wide Web: www.ivpress.com
E-mail: mail@ivpress.com

InterVarsity Press® is the book-publishing division of InterVarsity Christian Fellowship/USA®, a student movement active on campus at hundreds of universities, colleges and schools of nursing in the United States of America, and a member movement of the International Fellowship of Evangelical Students. For information about local and regional activities, write Public Relations Dept., InterVarsity Christian Fellowship/USA, 6400 Schroeder Rd., P.O. Box 7895, Madison, WI 53707-7895, or visit the IVCF website at <www.intervarsity.org>.

All Scripture quotations, unless otherwise indicated, are taken from the Holy Bible, New International Version®. NIV®. Copyright ©1973, 1978, 1984 by International Bible Society. Used by permission of Zondervan Publishing House. All rights reserved.

All extracts by C. S. Lewis copyright © C. S. Lewis Pte. Ltd. Reprinted by permission.

Design: Cindy Kiple
Images: Comstock Images/Getty Images

ISBNs   0-8308-3285-8
        978-0-8308-3285-9

Printed in the United States of America ∞

Library of Congress Cataloging-in-Publication Data

Lindsley, Arthur.
    C. S. Lewis's case for Christ: insights from reason, imagination
    and faith/Art Lindsley.
        P. cm.
    Includes bibliographical references (p.   ) and index.
    ISBN 0-8308-3285-8 (pbk.: alk. paper)
    1. Apologetics. 2. Lewis, C. S. (Clive Staples),
    1898-1963—religion. I. Title.
    BT1103.L56 2005
    239—dc22
                                                                    2005012105

| P | 18 | 17 | 16 | 15 | 14 | 13 | 12 | 11 | 10 | 9 | 8 | 7 | 6 | 5 | 4 | 3 | 2 |
| Y | 20 | 19 | 18 | 17 | 16 | 15 | 14 | 13 | 12 | 11 | 10 | 09 | 08 | 07 | 06 | 05 |

To Connie,

"An excellent wife, who can find?"
(Proverbs 31:10 NASB)

This book would not
have come into being without you.

CONTENTS

ACKNOWLEDGMENTS

Many people helped me in the process of writing this book. I want to thank the staff of Westmont College for allowing me to use their facilities during my sabbatical and, in particular, to thank Westmont Provost Shirley Mullen, President Stan Gaede, and library director John Murray. I also wish to thank the C. S. Lewis Institute for allowing me the use of material on C. S. Lewis, some of which first appeared in their publication *Knowing and Doing*. I thank you Dale and Sandy Larsen for editing the entire manuscript as well as expanding and adding to the dialogues at the beginning and ending of each chapter, which helped in making it a better book.

I am especially indebted to Becky Cooke for typing the manuscript through its many revisions and for all the time she freely donated to this effort. The Oasis Ministry board helped to finance my time to write *True Truth* and this book. Thanks go to Doug and Nancy Greenwold, Jim and Becky Cooke, Todd and Pam Ramsey, Ken and Caroline Broussard, and Bill and Marsha Nickels. Special thanks also go to faithful donors Kim and Kathy Cooke, Bob and Jean Baldwin, Harland and Sheila Buhler, Bob and Martha Haley, Gil and Ruth Emery, David Hinshelwood, Dennis and Karen Hogge, Wayne and Wendy Hughes, Shang Hsiung, Jack and Joanne Kemp, John and Alex

Mitchell, Wendy Verhof, and Rick and Dody Wellock.

Numerous people have read the manuscript and given comments. Jim Beavers spent much time editing and correcting my initial manuscript. C. S. Lewis experts Dr. Jerry Root and Dr. Chris Mitchell contributed their valuable comments. Dan Tagle and Bill Cron also gave helpful input.

Furthermore, I want to thank the staff of InterVarsity Press, particularly Gary Deddo, for all their help and encouragement to see this book published.

Last, but not by any means least, I want to thank my wife Connie for encouraging me in my vision to write and for making it possible for the sabbatical and summer times away. I thank the Lord for you, Connie.

PART ONE

WHY STUDY LEWIS'S CASE FOR CHRIST?

1

Why Consider C. S. Lewis's
Arguments for Christ?

✝

One by one, coffee mugs in hand, people begin to drift toward the carpeted corner of the bookstore where John stands waiting. He gets a hollow feeling in his stomach and unconsciously puts his hand on the stack of books on the table beside him. Their solid feel boosts his confidence. The spine of each book bears the name of the same author: C. S. Lewis. John wonders who will come to this first meeting of a study group on the thinking of a mid-twentieth-century British writer.

John is not afraid that C. S. Lewis will be irrelevant to anyone who comes tonight. He knows that the works of Lewis hold something for everyone. But what unpredictable mix of people will this study group draw? Will they be familiar with Lewis's works? Perhaps some will have read his fiction series for children, The Chronicles of Narnia, while others will know him for his writings on Christian faith. To some he may be only a half-familiar name, somebody from J. R. R. Tolkien's inner circle.

"How many chairs do you think you'll need?" A store employee's voice breaks into John's musings. John hurries to help the clerk arrange a circle *of chairs. Just in time—the first members of the group have arrived.*

"Good evening and welcome to this initial meeting of our study group on C. S. Lewis." John sounds more self-assured than he feels. "To help us get acquainted, please take one of these markers and write your first name on one of these sticky name tags."

When everyone has found a seat and has affixed a name tag, John says, "I'm curious about why we've all decided to be here this evening. Who would like to tell us why you're interested in the work and thought of C. S. Lewis?"

A woman who looks to be in her thirties immediately raises her hand and announces, "I'm Brenda." She hardly needs to say it, because her name is written large and bold, crowding the edges of the sticker. Brenda wears loud-colored, offbeat clothing and large "artsy" jewelery. "I want to write children's literature. Not sugary-sweet stuff, but stories that deal with the real world as kids experience it. I want to know how Lewis managed to write stories that speak to both children and adults."

A man about Brenda's age, but more conservative in appearance, speaks up. "My name is Simon and I'm an atheist." Simon flicks a glance around the circle as if to see if anyone is shocked, but no one visibly reacts. "It bothers me that so many people today are being taken in by religion. I heard that this guy, Lewis, was once a hard-core atheist. I want to know how such a seemingly intelligent person was duped into believing in a God."

A middle-aged woman raises her hand next and says firmly, "I'm Julia and I'm definitely not an atheist. I've been on a spiritual quest for several years. I don't restrict myself to any one religion. I investigate all spiritual paths and draw on each for what best fits my life. I'm here to see what I can glean from C. S. Lewis's brand of Christianity."

Next to speak is a woman who appears the youngest of the group. "I consider myself a Christian," she says. "I promised this friend of mine I'd come to this because she's always telling me I need to think more about my faith. But to me, faith is a matter of feeling, not thinking. Oh, by the way, my name's Lenae."

The rest of the group remains silent, perhaps intimidated by the reasons of the four who have spoken. Then an older man says, "I'm Mike and I'm just here for the coffee," and everyone laughs. John takes a deep breath and goes into his introduction to C. S. Lewis.

WHO WAS C. S. LEWIS?

In touch with real people. Like the members of John's study group, no doubt you have some degree of knowledge about Clive Staples Lewis, writer, teacher, thinker and above all Christian. Lewis was an Oxford professor who was born November 29, 1898, in Belfast, Northern Ireland. He died November 22, 1963, the same day John F. Kennedy was assassinated.

Because he was heard on regular BBC radio broadcasts during World War II, Lewis became well-known in Britain. It is said that he was the second best-known radio voice of that era; Winston Churchill was number one. Lewis received further exposure in America when he was pictured on the cover of *Time* magazine on September 8, 1947. The cover read: "Oxford's C. S. Lewis: His Heresy: Christianity."

Besides his many books defending and explaining his faith in Christ, Lewis also wrote fiction, science fiction, well-respected academic works in English literature, and poetry. Critics once predicted that Lewis's influence would diminish with time. Time has proven them wrong, and if anything, Lewis's popularity is growing. A recent poll of *Christianity Today* readers found that the book (other than the Bible) that has most influenced their lives was C. S. Lewis's *Mere Christianity.*[1]

Films such as the BBC and Hollywood versions of *Shadowlands* have revealed personal details of Lewis's life. The Hollywood version with Anthony Hopkins and Deborah Winger was especially emotionally powerful and was nominated for a couple of Academy Awards. While Lewis would likely be horrified to see his romance with Joy and his crushing grief at her death displayed on the silver screen, the films have nevertheless served as many people's entry point into the life and writing of C. S. Lewis. But even the popularity of these movies is easily dwarfed by the massive sales of a wide variety of his books.

What is the reason for the continuing popularity of one who to many is a relatively obscure English author? Lewis's unique combination of abilities set him apart from others. His gifts included an ability to combine story, imagination, metaphor and reason; the rhetorical skill to order his ideas clearly and persuasively; precision with words; and the empathy to understand people's deepest struggles, questions, and doubts. Better than many pastors and theologians, he was able to get in touch with the concerns of real people.

An ardent atheist. Apart from his fame and popularity, why should we give further consideration to Lewis's thought? One reason is that Lewis knew what it was like not to believe, because he struggled with many doubts along the way to faith. Since he was an ardent atheist until age thirty-one, his experience and education prepared him to understand firsthand the most common arguments against Christianity. Even after he came to belief in God, calling himself "the most dejected and reluctant convert in all of England,"[2] he took two years to sort out various competing religious claims, particularly between Eastern religious ideas (pantheism) and Christianity. Finally he became convinced of the truth of the Christian message.

Lewis's conversion to Christ was outwardly unspectacular. He describes a trip in the sidecar of a motorcycle on the way to the Whipsnade Zoo. When he left for the zoo, he did not believe that Christ was the Son of God; when he arrived at the zoo, he did believe that Christ was the Son of God. Otherwise nothing extraordinary had happened along the way.

Lewis's first book, *Pilgrim's Regress,* is particularly valuable because it describes some of the dilemmas he faced on his spiritual journey. Much like Pilgrim in John Bunyan's *Pilgrim's Progress,* Lewis's character, John, sets out on a quest. Rather than encountering generic temptations as in Bunyan's classic book, John meets characters who give philosophical alternatives to faith. Through this avenue Lewis highlights the arguments he himself had struggled with. He does not lightly dismiss crucial problems and obstacles to faith.

A thorough scholar. Lewis had an enormous breadth and depth of knowledge. His earlier studies gave him a mastery of philosophy, classics and literature. He accomplished the rare feat of getting three firsts at Oxford, including top honors in Greats and English. He lectured in philosophy for a year before he was elected a fellow in English at Magdalen College, Oxford, in 1925. Lewis taught there until 1954, when he was appointed professor of Medieval and Renaissance studies at Cambridge University. He mastered ancient, medieval, renaissance and reformation philosophy and literature. For example, his highly regarded book *English Literature in the Sixteenth Century* took him sixteen years to write because he felt he had to read everything in English in the sixteenth century before he wrote the book. This was typical of his thoroughness.

Of course certain areas of study lay outside his area of specialty, as he often admitted, but he was very aware of the philosophical, religious and literary debates which led up to his own time.

A debater. Lewis was not only aware of past debates, but he also engaged in the current debates of his age, many of which laid the groundwork for the controversies of our own time. For a number of years he served as an adviser and central voice at the Oxford Socratic Club. The group provided a forum for debate and discussion between leading advocates of Christianity and leading opponents of that belief (such as A. J. Ayer). Each meeting included a presentation of a paper or talk from one side or the other and then a response from the opposing side, followed by general discussion. C. S. Lewis was sometimes a presenter or respondent, but even if neither, he was invariably a significant presence in the later discussion.

Austin Farrer, well-known philosopher and warden of Keble College, Oxford, maintains that Lewis's great value was his "many-sidedness" and that he was a "bonny fighter." When Farrer spoke at the Socratic Club, he often went with fear and trembling that he would not be adequate to the discussion that would follow. He wrote, "But there Lewis would be, sniffing the imminent battle and saying 'Aha!' at the sound of the trumpet. My anxieties rolled away. Whatever ineptitudes I might commit, he would maintain the cause; and nobody could put Lewis down."[3]

There is only one known exception to Lewis's formidable defense, and even the exception proves the rule. In one instance when one of his arguments in his book *Miracles* was questioned, he admitted it needed clarification, which was news, a shock to some of those present. He made the clarification in future editions of the book.

Intellectual genius. Many people who met Lewis can vouch for the quality of his intellect. He debated successfully with the best thinkers of the land because he had an almost instant recall of what he read. Lewis said that he was "cursed" with not being able to forget anything that he read.

Sometimes in his rooms at Oxford, Lewis would play a parlor game, asking a visitor to pull any book out of his extensive library and read aloud a few lines. Lewis would then proceed to quote the rest of the poetry or prose verbatim for pages. For instance, Kenneth Tynan, who became a well-known English dramatist and critic, told of an encounter with Lewis during a tutorial at Oxford. Tynan said, "He had the most astonishing memory of any man I have ever known. In conversation I might have said to him, 'I read a marvelous medieval poem this morning and I particularly liked this line.' I would then quote the line. Lewis would usually go on to quote the rest of the page. It was astonishing.

> "Once when I was invited to his rooms after dinner for a glass of beer, he played a game. He directed, 'Give me a number from one to forty.' I said, 'Thirty.'
>
> "He acknowledged, 'Right, go to the thirtieth shelf in my library.' Then he said, 'Give me another number from one to twenty.'
>
> "I answered, 'Fourteen.'
>
> "He continued, 'Right. Get the fourteenth book off the shelf. Now let's have a number from one to one hundred.'
>
> "I said, 'Forty-six.'
>
> "'Now turn to page forty-six. Pick a number from one to twenty-five for the line of the page.'
>
> "I said, 'Six.'
>
> "'So,' he would say, 'read me that line.' He could always identify it—not only by identifying the book, but he was also usually able to quote the rest of the page. This is a gift. This is something you cannot learn. It was remarkable."[4]

Dean John Leyerle, professor of English at the University of Toronto, was another witness to Lewis's amazing memory. At a farewell dinner when Lewis left Oxford for Cambridge, Lewis commented to Richard Selig, an American Rhodes Scholar, "The difficulty is that I remember everything I've ever read and bits pop up uninvited."

"Surely not everything you've ever read, Mr. Lewis?"

"Yes, everything, Selig, even the most boring texts."

By now the end of the table was silent and waiting to see if Selig would drop the matter, but he backed off very little. Selig got to his feet and went to the college library, which was open late in the term, and took out a volume of a long and little-read poem. He returned and opened the volume. He read a few lines. "'Stop!' said Lewis who lifted his eyes toward the ceiling and began to recite the poem in a rich and modulated public voice. He stopped after ten lines or so and looked at Selig, now very silent. Conversation was slow to resume at that end of the table."[5]

Such an all-inclusive memory, combined with vast rhetorical gifts, caused most Lewis critics to launch their disparaging remarks from a distance. The risk in a face-to-face encounter was too great.

Lifelong friendships. C. S. Lewis was not just an ivory-tower scholar, all head and no heart. He had a warm, engaging personality, made deep, lifelong friendships, and possessed a lively sense of humor.

Lewis's stepson Douglas Gresham recalls that to be around Lewis was to be in the presence of laughter. His great sense of humor was one of the traits that most endeared him to his friends and acquaintances.[6]

Lewis made and kept many lifelong friends. Even when he became a believer in Christ, he did not walk away from his friends who now disagreed with him. For example, throughout his life he continued to correspond with his childhood friend Arthur Greeves. Greeves was a believer in Christ when Lewis was an atheist; later when Lewis became a believer, Greeves lost his earlier faith. Nevertheless Lewis continued to pour out his love for Arthur Greeves. That was his attitude toward other friends as well.

At Oxford Lewis was often surrounded by a group of friends who referred to themselves as the "Inklings." They got together twice weekly, usually Tuesday mornings and Thursday evenings. The morning meetings were often at a local pub—the Eagle and Child— and the evening meetings in Lewis's rooms at Magdalen College. Since there was no formal membership, many people attended over the years, but some of the regulars included Charles Williams, Warren Lewis (C. S. Lewis's brother), and J. R. R. Tolkien.

Tolkien was instrumental in Lewis's coming to faith in Christ. In 1927 Tolkien invited Lewis to join the Coalbiters Club, which focused on reading Icelandic myths. These and other regular meetings allowed Tolkien and Lewis (still an atheist at that time) to talk about issues related to faith. In 1929 Lewis embraced faith in God, and in 1931 he came to believe in Christ as the Son of God. Tolkien met with Lewis many times during this period and contributed greatly to Lewis's spiritual quest. They remained close, lifelong friends.

The sharp clarity of Lewis's thinking came partly from his constant interaction with world-class minds who showed him omissions in his perspective and sharpened his ability to put forward what he believed. Dr. Jim Houston (founder of Regent College in Vancouver, British Columbia, and of the C. S. Lewis Institute in Washington, D.C.) knew Lewis while both taught at Oxford. Dr. Houston writes:

> What really gave Lewis his skill, I think, was that he went out of his way far more than the rest of his colleagues to share his writings with his friends. One of the things that give such quality to Lewis's work is that his statements were like diamonds with many facets, coming no doubt from a good deal of discussion, of arguing together.[7]

Powerful communicator. C. S. Lewis was able to communicate powerfully not only in the written word but also in the spoken word. His lectures were always well-attended. When he preached at the University Church (St. Mary's) you had to get there early to get a seat. As he became more well-known, especially after his BBC addresses, he was in much demand as a speaker. During World War II he often spoke on Royal Air Force bases to soldiers flying hazardous duty. The average life span of pilots was thirteen trips across the English Channel before they were shot down or listed as missing in action. At one such base, Stuart Barton Babbage (later an author and vice president of a seminary) describes Lewis's talk given one evening:

> His style of speaking was personal rather than oratorical. He spoke earnestly and emphatically. In this address, we were, once again, made aware of his extraordinary feeling for words, of his rare ability to use exactly the right word in the right place, and of the endless fertility of his imagination. . . . Lewis had the gift of natural eloquence in abundant measure. Like the Roman orator of antiquity, he was eager to present his case, to plead its merits, and to demand a verdict.[8]

C. S. Lewis's "consummate skill" and combination of intellectual genius, breadth of learning, and powerful communication skills make him someone worth listening to, even if we, in the end, disagree with him.[9]

CLUES TO THE COSMOS

Like a great detective, C. S. Lewis helps us put together clues to the cosmos. Detective stories always offer clues that the hero pursues to find out "who done it?" Sometimes we can figure out who did the crime before someone like Sherlock Holmes does. More often we miss certain clues or fail to see the implications of the ones we are given. Holmes might consider it all "elementary," but the rest of us need Holmes's help to put it all together.

A person comes to believe, not when one thing seems to prove that faith is credible but when everything confirms the teachings of that faith. Lewis examined all of life, reason, imagination, experience and practice (personal and social) for clues to the cosmos. Lewis's defense of his faith involved not simply a few isolated arguments but a comprehensive sense in which faith in Christ fits everything.

To use another analogy, have you ever searched for the right key to open a lock, trying every key on a ring crammed with keys of all shapes and sizes? The frustrating hunt resembles our search through various religious views we encounter. Does any one view fit better than any of the others? Is there one that unlocks the lock?

Lewis came to the conviction that Jesus Christ was the key to unlock the mysteries of life. He said, "I believe in Christianity as I believe that the sun has risen, not only because I see it, but because by it I see everything else."[10]

So why should anyone—believer or nonbeliever—study C. S. Lewis's case for Christ?

- Lewis's writings have had a greater effect on believers in the latter part of the twentieth century than any book other than the Bible.

- He had a unique ability to combine reason and imagination.

- He was a committed unbeliever for many years, so he knows the arguments and the feelings against Christianity.

- His breadth of knowledge and his intellectual genius class him among the most brilliant people to have examined the Christian faith.

- His views were tested and refined by his interaction with top opponents of the faith in his day and with other deep thinkers whom he allowed to critique his work.

- His personal qualities made him one who was capable of warmth, loyal friendship and laughter. His writings engage but never try to coerce.

At this point you may ask, Why should I read a book *about* C. S. Lewis? Why not read Lewis himself? Good question! If you have not read *Mere Christianity* and you are inclined to do so, put this book down immediately and begin. *Mere Christianity* is a great introduction to Lewis's thought and is one of his most accessible and helpful books. I hope that this study will not be a substitute for reading Lewis but, rather, that it will encourage you to begin the journey.

NOT AN INFALLIBLE GURU

As John's overview of Lewis winds down, Brenda shoots up her hand and comments sharply, "You make it sound like Lewis could do no wrong. Didn't he have any detractors?"

"Of course," John replies. "Lewis had many critics, and he still does today. When he presented classic beliefs about Christ, he got intensely negative reactions from atheists"—John glances toward Simon, who smiles a little—"and even from other Christians less confident of the truth of their faith."

Brenda persists, "So who were those critics? What were some of the holes they punched in his arguments?"

"Well, a couple in modern times have been philosopher John Beversluis and biographer A. N. Wilson. I don't think their criticisms hurt C. S. Lewis's case for Christ, and there have been a number of solid responses to what they wrote."

Mike interrupts, "Hey, aren't we getting ahead of things? How can we talk about criticisms of Lewis until we know what he believed in the first place?"

"I thought you were just here for the coffee," Lenae points out.

John smiles and says, "You know, Mike's right. Before we can intelligently decide whether we agree with Lewis, we need to be sure we understand what he believed and how he got there."

Lenae looks genuinely puzzled. "What does it matter whether we agree with him? If his religion worked for him, then it was valid for him. Doesn't mean it has to be valid for you or me or any of us."

"Hang onto that thought, Lenae," John advises. "I guarantee we'll be talking about that question later. For now, let's take a look at Lewis's spiritual journey."

Julia speaks up. "OK, but only as long as you don't try to make him into some kind of infallible guru."

"No chance of that, Julia," John assures her. "C. S. Lewis was just as flawed and human as the rest of us. The obstacles to faith which he struggled over are not so different from the ones we face. Let's talk about them."

WHAT WERE LEWIS'S OBSTACLES TO FAITH?

John looks around at the faces of the people in his C. S. Lewis study group. Not everyone has spoken up yet. He hopes that the next part of the study will spur everyone to join the discussion. "Remember that at one time Lewis was an atheist. Simon, you probably think he should have remained one."

Simon gives a brief, curt nod. Julia suggests, "So at that point he was openly hostile to religion. I can understand that. I was at that point a few years ago."

"I don't know if hostility is the best word to describe his attitude," John answers carefully, "but yes, he was intellectually convinced of his atheism. He expressed his convictions in letters and in conversations with Christians he met."

Brenda says, "OK, let's hear it! I want to know all of Lewis's reasons not to believe in God."

"Well, like many people in Britain at that time, Lewis started out early with a nominal Christian faith. But several significant—even traumatic—

events in his life became obstacles to faith, until he rejected not only Christianity but belief in any god. Let's look at some of those events."

C. S. LEWIS'S PAIN IN EARLY LIFE

Lewis had one sibling, Warren, who was three years older and with whom he remained friends all his life. Lewis's earliest memories involve "endless books" in the study, dining room, cloakroom, bedrooms and piled as high as his shoulder in the attic. On the often-dreary days, time would be spent in reading and in imaginative games involving "dressed animals" and "knights in armor." These were the subjects of Lewis's first novel, *Boxen,* which he wrote at the age of twelve.

The most shattering event of Lewis's early life was the death of his mother when he was nine years old. Lewis says in his autobiography, *Surprised by Joy,* "With my mother's death all settled happiness disappeared from my life. There was much fun, many pleasures, many stabs of joy; but no more of the old security. It was sea and islands now; the great continent had sunk like Atlantis."[1] At this point he lost not only his mother but also, in effect, his father. Albert Lewis became emotionally withdrawn and decided to send both sons to boarding school, an experience that proved very difficult for both boys. Warren Lewis later wrote, "With his uncanny flair for making the wrong decision, my father had given us helpless children into the hands of a madman."[2] The boarding school's headmaster, whom the students called "Oldie," inflicted harsh punishment on those who failed their lessons. He was later declared insane, and the school was closed.

Problems with prayer. During this period Lewis attended church and attempted to take the Christian faith seriously. He tried to pray every night but developed what he describes as a "false conscience" about prayer. He had been told that it was not enough to say your prayers; you also had to think about what you were saying. As soon as he finished his prayers each night, he would ask himself, "Are you sure you were thinking about what you were saying?" The answer was inevitably no. Then he would say his prayers again, sometimes multiple times. The result was insomnia and nightly torment. Lewis wrote, "Had I pursued the same road much further, I think I should have gone mad."[3] Lewis later wrote about the difficulties of prayer in *Letters to Malcolm.*

Unbelief confirmed. At Chartres, a later boarding school, one of Lewis's teachers introduced him to the occult. He also began to grapple with doubts about God, which rose from the problem of evil in the world and from what he perceived as the similarity between Christianity and paganism. In addition, he struggled with sexual temptation. The toxic combination of inner and outer pressures led to the loss of whatever faith he might have had. He had lost not only his faith but his virtue and simplicity. (Years later, after he came to faith in Christ, he rid himself of unchastity, atheism and the occult but remained subject to one acquired habit: smoking.)[4]

Chronological snobbery. One factor that worked against faith in Lewis's mind and heart was what he later called his "chronological snobbery." By that he meant "the uncritical acceptance of the intellectual climate of our own age and the assumption that whatever has gone out of date is on that count discredited." Lewis's friend Owen Barfield helped Lewis dismantle his prejudice against old ideas by arguing that if an idea seems outdated, we must ask, "Why did it go out of date?" and "Was it ever refuted (by whom, where, and how conclusively)?"[5] Later in his life, Lewis directly and indirectly took on chronological snobbery.

Problem of evil. Lewis's struggle with the problem of evil persisted until his conversion and even beyond. These lines from Lucretius echo Lewis's own quandary:

> Had God designed the world, it would not be
> A world as frail and faulty as we see.[6]

While Lewis eventually arrived at an intellectual resolution of the difficulty, the emotional struggle continued, especially at the death of his wife, Joy. He describes his intellectual wrestling in *The Problem of Pain,* and his emotional struggle in *A Grief Observed.*

Parallel mythologies. At the time and place of Lewis's education, classic Christianity was the dominant worldview. It was assumed that pagan religions and mythologies were interesting but false, while Christianity, though similar to them in many ways, was true. Lewis dared to wonder, on what grounds should Christianity be exempt from the verdict of "false"? Why was *this* religion—and this one *alone*—true?

The problem of similar mythologies remained an obstacle for Lewis right up until his conversion. As we will see later, a discussion with J. R. R. Tolkien was instrumental in resolving this conflict. Lewis later wrote about myth in a number of his nonfiction works and in one of his novels, *Till We Have Faces.*

Immersion in rationalism. When he was sixteen, Lewis was tutored by a brilliant teacher named W. T. Kirkpatrick. "Kirk," or the "Great Knock" as he was also called, taught Lewis to analyze, think, write and speak clearly and logically.

When they first met at the train station, young Jack (as he chose to call himself) commented to Kirk that he had not expected the wildness of the scenery of Surrey. "Stop," said Kirk. "What do you mean by wildness and what grounds do you have for not expecting it?" As Jack attempted to answer, it became increasingly clear that he had no distinct idea about the word *wildness* and that "insofar as I had any idea at all, wildness was a singularly inept word." "Do you not see," concluded the Great Knock, "that your remark was meaningless?" Thinking that the subject had been dropped, Jack proceeded to sulk. Never was he more mistaken. Kirk inquired about the basis of Jack's expectations of the flora and geology of Surrey. Kirk concluded, "Do you not see then, that you had no right to have any opinion whatever on the subject?" It had never occurred to Jack that his thoughts needed to be based on anything.[7]

Such rigorous interrogation set the tone of his tutelage under Kirk, and it was of immeasurable benefit to Lewis. Much of the clarity of his writing, his careful choice of words, his well-considered arguments for the faith and his later tutorial style were shaped during this period. Lewis says: "My debt to him is very great, my reverence to this day undiminished."[8] Some have said that Lewis wrote many of his later works with a sense that Kirk (although by that time dead) was looking over his shoulder.

Kirk was an atheist and a rationalist. Lewis called him nearly "a purely logical entity."[9] Although he never attacked religion in Jack's presence, his rigorous rationalism (of the nineteenth-century type) reinforced and provided ammunition for Lewis's unbelief. Kirk might have provided inspiration for such characters as Mr. Enlightenment in *Pilgrim's Regress* or McPhee in *That Hideous Strength*. Later, Lewis critiqued rationalism—now called modernism—in *Pilgrim's Regress* and in other writings.

Imagination versus reason. Loving literature as he did, Lewis was forced to consider the tension between his atheism and all the poetry and novels that wrestled with the questions of meaning, dignity, truth, goodness, beauty and immortality. He came to believe philosophically that the universe was a grim and meaningless place, yet in his imagination he yearned for the satisfaction of the deep human aspirations he found in literature. A contradiction emerged between his reason and his imagination. Was his reason right and the longings evoked by his imagination meaningless? Or was his imagination right when it pointed to real satisfaction for human aspirations, and his atheism wrong? He resolved this tension in *Surprised by Joy.*

As one of his first steps in his journey to faith, Lewis identifies a time when his imagination was baptized. It occurred while he was reading a copy of George MacDonald's *Phantastes* on a train ride. As he read, a "new quality" touched his life, what he described at first as a "bright shadow," but later came to realize was "holiness." That night his imagination was "baptized," although, he says, "the rest of me not unnaturally took longer."[10]

Later Lewis came to see imagination as a key to the meaning of the cosmos. We will look at the prominent place of imagination in his view of life and see how his fiction, as much as his nonfiction, points to Christ.

Disbelief in miracles. During his atheist years Lewis simply assumed that miracles do not happen and that it would be naive and unsophisticated to think they do. He was shocked to learn that Neville Coghill and J. R. R. Tolkien, some of the most intelligent and best-informed people he knew, were supernaturalists—that is, they believed that there is more to the universe than the natural world we see and experience. Even more stunning to Lewis was a fireside comment by one of the most hard-boiled atheists he knew: that the "historicity of the gospels was really surprisingly good." The atheist referred to pagan mythology of a "dying god" who rose again, then mused, "It almost looks as if it really happened once." The impact of this statement on Lewis was immense. If this militant unbeliever, the "toughest of the toughs," was not safe, where could Lewis turn? Was there no escape?[11] Lewis was forced to reexamine his antisupernatural assumptions. He later wrote about miracles in a number of his essays and in his book *Miracles*.

OBSTACLES OVERCOME

One by one, Lewis's arguments against God were countered and his obstacles to faith were knocked down. Already his imagination had been "baptized" and his reason satisfied. He felt the "steady, unrelenting approach of Him whom I so desperately desired not to meet"[12] until he came to believe in God and ultimately to believe in Christ as the Son of God.

In his writings Lewis does not develop his defense of faith in a systematic fashion. Rather he writes about the obstacles that once stood in the way of faith for him. The issues that stood in the way of his belief in God have also been stumbling blocks for many of his readers, which is one reason so many people from various backgrounds resonate with Lewis.

In summary, some of the factors that led Lewis into unbelief were

• early pain over the loss of his mother

• difficulties with prayer

• chronological snobbery

• the problem of evil in the world

• parallels between mythology and Christianity

• indoctrination into rationalism

• tension between reason and imagination

• disbelief in miracles

THE SAME TODAY

Lenae quietly observes, "He sure went through a lot when he was young. But didn't he kind of overdo some of those obstacles? I'm not sure I got the part about mythology."

Julia says, "I think I got it, but I don't see why it was such an obstacle. Why shouldn't different religions use some of the same images and symbols?"

"Especially when they're all meaningless anyway," Simon adds.

John sees that he needs to jump in quickly. "Lewis came to some interesting conclusions about mythology—with the help of Tolkien, by the way. We'll get into that a little later. But what do you think of his obstacles to faith? Have any of you faced the same obstacles?"

For a moment the group is quiet. Then John is startled to hear a new voice. It comes from a man apparently in his forties. "I've only read Lewis's fiction. I didn't know anything about his life. It seems he and I have some things in common. I lost my parents when I was ten. At the time I asked God a lot of questions and felt like I didn't get any answers. Now I don't know if there's a God or not. I've tried not to think about it much, but . . ." His voice trails off.

John squints at the man's name tag. "Thank you, . . ."

"Damon."

Julia says, "Maybe there's a reason for your being here, Damon." John silently agrees.

PART TWO

OBSTACLES TO FAITH

3

CHRONOLOGICAL SNOBBERY

What Does a Two-Thousand-Year-Old
Religion Have to Do with Me?

A week has gone by. It's time for the second meeting of the Lewis study group, and John hopes everyone will show up. He is not disappointed.

Brenda arrives first. She has voiced strong opinions, but so far she has said nothing about children's literature, supposedly her main motive for coming. Damon, who finally spoke up last week, arrives next, followed by Simon the atheist. (John warns himself, I've got to stop thinking of him as just "the atheist.") Mike arrives next. It's obvious by now that he is here for more than the coffee. He is followed by Julia, the one on a spiritual quest. Just as John is about to get started, Lenae rushes in, gasping apologies about work and traffic and last-minute phone calls.

John begins with a question. "Is anybody here old-fashioned?" A ripple of discomfort moves around the circle. Mike, the oldest one there, responds, "I'd say I'm old-fashioned about some things. Morality, for example."

"Thanks, Mike. Most of us cringe at the idea of being thought old-

fashioned. But C. S. Lewis would ask us, why do we assume that newer is better? He had a name for that assumption: chronological snobbery."

"Newer is better," says Lenae, who has caught her breath. "A newer car is better than an older car." At some cynical snorts from the others, she admits, "Well, I guess it depends on the car. But I wouldn't want to go back to the days before cars and electricity and computers—would you?"

"I'd like to go back before cell phones," says Simon. "I almost got run down the other day. Some idiot was talking on the phone and driving and eating—all at the same time."

Once again John has to jump in. "Do you notice how, when we think of new versus old, right away we start to talk about inventions? Lewis said that just because newer machines—today we'd say newer technology—are better, we shouldn't assume that everything newer is better."

Immediately Brenda demands, "So what are some old things that Lewis would say are better? Oh, never mind, I know what you're going to say. Religion, right?"

"You're on the right track, Brenda."

Julia says, "Religion doesn't have to mean old religion. I happen to think the world needs a new religion, a faith for now, something that works in today's world."

Lenae nods her head in vigorous agreement. "Yeah, the Bible was written thousands of years ago. Nobody back then knew about black holes or the size of the universe. And as for morality, who can say anymore what's right and wrong? It's all a matter of your cultural background. No offense, Mike."

Damon says, "A new religion could still have some Christian elements like—I don't know, love your neighbor and treat people fairly—but it wouldn't have to have the old idea of God on a big throne up in the sky."

John raises both hands. "Hold on. Before we talk about specifics,

*whether it's cars or religion or cell phones, let's look at how Lewis dealt with
the wider issue of chronological snobbery."*

A ROTTEN EGG

Like some of the members of the study group, and like many twentieth-century people, C. S. Lewis wondered how an ancient religion
could have anything to do with now. Wasn't Christianity old-fashioned, outmoded, a relic of the past? And what did twentieth-century
people do with outmoded ideas? They threw them out like anything
else that had outlived its usefulness. The charge that Christianity is
out of date has only gotten louder in the twenty-first century.

In numerous discussions with his friend Owen Barfield, Lewis
wrestled with the idea that Christian faith was outmoded. Barfield
did not reject Lewis's uncertainty; rather, he helped Lewis go beyond
it. Lewis came to understand that his question raised further questions that needed to be answered before he could reach a decision
about Christianity or about any "old" idea.

What were those further questions? Barfield said that for any supposedly outmoded idea, we must inquire along these lines:

• Why did this idea go out of date?

• Was the idea ever refuted?

• If it was refuted, by whom, where and how conclusively?[1]

If we are inclined to reject an idea, we must first take time to determine whether it is really false. We would not want to say that everything ancient peoples believed was false. Then which of their beliefs were false, and why? More important, which of their beliefs
remain true?

Lewis later labeled his own attitude "chronological snobbery." He
defined it as "the uncritical acceptance of the intellectual climate of

our own age and the assumption that whatever has gone out of date is on that count discredited."[2] In other words, we take for granted that the prevailing ideas of our time and culture are unquestionably true.

In *The Voyage of the Dawn Treader,* the fifth book in the Chronicles of Narnia series, King Caspian encounters Gumpas, the governor of the Lone Islands. Gumpas tells Caspian that the slave trade practiced in his domain is "an essential part of the development of the island." Caspian objects to the practice. Gumpas counters his objection by claiming that all the economic indicators prove his case, and he has statistics and graphs to back it up.

> "Tender as my years may be," said Caspian, "I believe I understand the slave trade from within quite as well as your Sufficiency. And I do not see that it brings into the islands meat or bread or beer or wine or timber or cabbages or books or instruments of music or horses or armor or anything else worth having. But, whether it does or not, it must be stopped."
>
> "But that would be putting the clock back," gasped the Governor. "Have you no idea of progress, of development?"
>
> "I have seen them both in an egg," said Caspian. "We call it going bad in Narnia. This trade must stop."[3]

Caspian's response reflects Lewis's contention that not all progress is good. Some new developments should be resisted. The newly developed slave trade, though supposedly economically beneficial, had to be stopped on the basis of higher, ethical grounds. It was progress in a direction that led to rottenness.

THE BREEZE OF THE CENTURIES

C. S. Lewis pointed out that his age, like past ages, had its own peculiar illusions and self-deceptions. The same is true today. Surrounded by the assumptions of our cultural environment, we may leave them unexamined and stay unaware of their impact on us. Colossians 2:8 cautions us not to be taken captive "through hollow and deceptive philosophy." Some believers take the warning to mean that they should avoid the subject of philosophy altogether. However, the passage actually points in the opposite direction, since the only way to beware of philosophy is to be aware of it. Otherwise, the untaught person may be captured by a new, "progressive" but rotten system of belief.

We need the help of the past to more accurately understand our own times. Earlier cultures did not share all our assumptions about the universe. As we read old books, we gain a different vantage point from which we see the assumptions of our time more clearly. Lewis urged us to deliberately read old books in order to let the "clean sea breeze of the centuries" blow through our minds. He made it a general rule that one should read as many old books as new ones:

> It's a good rule after reading a new book never to allow yourself another new one till you have read an old one in between. If that is too much for you, you should at least read one old one to three new ones. . . . Every age has its own outlook. It is especially good for seeing certain truths and especially liable to make certain mistakes. We all therefore need the books that will correct the characteristic mistakes of our own period. . . . None of us can fully escape this blindness, but we shall certainly increase it, and weaken our guard against it, if we read only modern books. . . . The only palliative is to keep the clean sea breeze of the centuries blowing through our minds and this can only be done by reading old books.[4]

GO BACK TO GO FORWARD

Sometimes we need to go back in order to go forward. G. K. Chesterton said, "Real development is not leaving things behind, as on a road, but drawing life from them, as from a root."[5] Some would object that looking backward for wisdom is like turning back the clock to an earlier century. Lewis answers this objection:

> As to putting the clock back, would you think I was joking if I said that you can put a clock back, and that if it is wrong it is often a very sensible thing to do? But I would rather get away from the whole idea of clocks. We all want progress. But progress means getting nearer to the place you want to be and if you have taken a wrong turning, then to go forward does not get you any nearer. If you are on the wrong road, progress means doing an about-turn and walking back to the right road; and in that case, the man who turns back soonest is the most progressive man. We have seen this when we do arithmetic. When I have started a sum the wrong way, the sooner I admit this and go back and start over again, the faster I shall get on. There is nothing progressive about being pigheaded and refusing to admit a mistake. And I think if you look at the present state of the world, it is pretty plain that humanity has been making some big mistakes. We are on the wrong road. And if this is so, we must go back. Going back is the quickest way on.[6]

Certainly it is never wise to go back to the past simply for its own sake. History provides bad examples as well as good. The past sometimes shows us how to live and sometimes how not to live. The classic proverb holds true: If we do not learn from history's mistakes, we are bound to repeat them. Where history does provide a good and worthy example, we must preserve and pass on the teachings of the past.

Jesus said that "every teacher of the law who has been instructed about the kingdom of heaven is like the owner of a house who brings out of his storeroom new treasures as well as old" (Matthew 13:52). Like the wise householder, we need to sift through our heritage, discard what was bad and pass on a good inheritance to future generations. As in everything else Christ is our perfect example here. Christ was not a wild-eyed revolutionary who sought to overthrow everything in the established religious order of his day. Neither was he a hidebound conservative who held fast to all the traditional practices; although there was much that he did want to conserve, particularly the truth of Scripture.

ENSLAVED TO THE RECENT PAST

Whether we like it or not, the past will affect us. The question is, which past: the recent past or the more distant past? Much of what masquerades as the newest, most novel philosophies of our time are actually a legacy of the past—not the distant past but the recent past. C. S. Lewis points out in his essay "On the Transmission of Christianity" that "the sources of unbelief among young people of today do not lie in those young people. The outlook they have—until they are taught better—is a backwash from an earlier period. It is nothing intrinsic to themselves that holds them back from the Faith."[7]

The teachers in Lewis's time were products of the post-World War I period. The prevailing beliefs of that time were passed on to those in the 1960s. The beliefs of the sixties (with some changes) tend to be the views passed on today and so on. Lewis says: "This very obvious fact—that each generation is taught by an earlier generation—must be kept firmly in mind. . . . The moment we forget this, we begin to talk nonsense about education."[8]

Even more than the general spirit of the times, the attitude and disposition of the teacher is passed on to the student. The cynical and suspicious mood of postmodernism tends to produce cynical suspicious students. Lewis maintains: "None can give another what he does not possess himself. No generation can bequeath to its successor what it has not got. . . . If we are skeptical we shall teach skepticism to our pupils, if fools only folly, if vulgar only vulgarity, if saints sanctity, if heroes heroism."[9]

Much of contemporary educational theory is guilty of an advanced form of chronological snobbery, arising from the 1960s-era rejection of basic cultural values and the overthrow of anything traditional. It not only rejects the values of the past, it claims that the study of history is itself pointless. According to this view, when we read the writings of the past, they do not tell us what really happened long ago; they only reveal the cultural bias of the writers and the political and social power structures in operation at the time of the writing. Therefore we can know nothing for sure about the past. And if we cannot know anything about the past, how can it guide us today?

THE DINOSAUR

C. S. Lewis was not afraid to be called old-fashioned, outdated or even a dinosaur. Lewis gave a classic talk titled "De Descriptione Temporium" as his inaugural address to his professorship at Cambridge. Toward the end of his address, Lewis claimed to be part of the old Western order more than the present post-Christian one. He acknowledged that while his outlook might seem to disqualify him from having anything important to say, it could also be a very positive qualification. He admitted, "You don't want to be lectured on Neanderthal Man by a Neanderthaler, still less on dinosaurs by a dinosaur."[10] On the other hand, Lewis argued, a dinosaur lecture might tell us some things we would like to know, especially since we have never seen a live dinosaur. He explained:

> If a live dinosaur dragged its slow length to the laboratory, would we not all look back as we fled? What a chance to know at last how it really moved and looked and smelled and what noises it made! And if the Neanderthaler could talk, then, though his lecturing technique might leave much to be desired, should we not almost certainly learn from him some things about him that the best modern anthropologist could never have told us? He would tell us without knowing he was telling.[11]

Lewis claimed that he read ancient texts as a native would read them rather than as a foreigner might. He suggested that "where I fail as a critic, I may yet be useful as a specimen. I would dare to go further. . . . I would say, use your specimen while you can. There are not going to be many more dinosaurs."[12]

THE TEMPTATION TO NOVELTY

No matter what period of history we live in or consider, those things that are most relevant will always be the things that are unchanging and eternal. Lewis called them "first things" or permanent things. Chronological snobs that most of us are, we find it difficult to believe that the newest may not be the best. We focus too much on the past twenty-four hours, the last week, the last month or the last year and not enough on that which lasts forever.

In his Cambridge address Lewis pointed to the temptation of the constant drive for novelty. For us today the problem is more complicated than ever. Inundated with gadgets that do everything faster and better, we become accustomed to snapping up every new technology. If I listed the latest ones here, they would soon sound antiquated as a newer list superseded them.

Lewis admitted that new technology offers real advantages over the old, but he refused to carry the analogy to all areas of life:

> In the world of machines the new is most often really better and the primitive really is the clumsy. And this image, potent in all our minds, reigns almost without rival in the minds of the uneducated. . . . [O]ur assumption that everything is provisional and soon to be superseded, that the attainment of goods we have never yet had, rather than the defense of and conservation of those we have already, is the cardinal business of life, would shock and bewilder them [people of the past] if they could visit [our time].[13]

The desire for the newest and latest is a powerful drive not only in twenty-first-century technology; it drives the realm of ideas and values as well. We are pulled to follow the newest philosophy, devour the latest books and ideas, and even come up with a radically innovative perspective of our own.

Theologian Thomas Oden is a model of the "temptation to novelty." Earlier in his life he was a respected, published liberal theologian. He tended to follow the newest fashion in religious theory. Then he had a revelation when he was about to leave on a sabbatical and could take only a limited number of books. He was shocked when he looked at the books he had chosen. None of the newest fad theologies were included—only old classics.

Gradually Oden worked his way back to what C. S. Lewis called "mere Christianity" or what Vincent of Lérins called that which is held "everywhere, always and by all." Oden had a dream that gave him a dramatic insight. He dreamed that he saw his own tombstone, and on it was written "He contributed nothing new." Most of us would interpret that as a posthumous insult! Instead, Oden came to see that the drive for novelty had consumed him. He determined in his life and his new theology series to "teach nothing new."[14] He found it necessary to resist the thrust of his education and "to overcome the constant temptation to novelty."[15]

An ancient proverb maintains that "what is true is not new and what is new is not true." While we can and should unearth new insights into truth, we should be cautious if we start to depart from the ideas believed and taught by Christians throughout history. Perhaps some traditional ideas need to be revised, and we are the ones to do it. However, if we differ greatly from the faithful giants of history, we must stay open to the possibility that it is we, not they, who need correction.

It is best not to value novelty or originality above everything else. It is certainly worthwhile to contribute a new perspective in our field of study or work. But Lewis warns against the assumption that to be "original" is the main purpose of life. He says: "No man who values originality will ever be original. But to try to tell the truth as you see it, try to do any bit of work as well as it can be done for the work's sake and what men call originality will come unsought."[16] Originality is best pursued indirectly, by doing good work rather than as an end in itself.

So in answer to those who call faith in Christ outmoded, old-fashioned, medieval, ancient, Victorian or modernist, I believe Lewis would reply along these lines: "You know, maybe I am a dinosaur. I certainly maintain that the truth I hold to is not new." Then he would ask us to consider these questions:

- Do you hold to a "chronological snobbery" that denies that any past belief could be true?

- If you reject certain "old-fashioned" views, have they ever been proved false? If so, where and how conclusively?

- Will you admit that our own period might have illusions and blind spots?

- Should we not "turn back the clock" when it is telling the wrong time?

- Are not the most modern and postmodern views really enslaved to the recent past?

- Perhaps I am a dinosaur, but would you not listen a while to a dinosaur if you could?

- Even if the latest might be the best in technology, is it necessarily best with respect to the true, the good and the beautiful, and especially with the eternal, unchanging God?

Finally I believe Lewis would say, "If you take your stand on the prevalent view, how long do you think it will prevail? . . . All you can say about my view is that it is old-fashioned; yours will soon be the same."[17] To put it another way, "All that is not eternal is eternally out of date."[18]

Sometimes we need to go full speed astern in order to go forward. If we see that we have begun wrongly, we must start over, not only in the realm of ideas but also in our personal life. C. S. Lewis says that this "full speed astern" movement is "what Christians call repentance."[19]

THE TEST OF TIME

"Well, that's one way I definitely agree with C. S. Lewis."

John is surprised. "How's that, Simon?"

"He said sometimes we need to turn back the clock because people were wiser in the past. I believe the human race should go back to the time before we fell into superstition about gods and a spirit world."

Mike says, with a bit of a put-on drawl, "You'd have to go back a long way. If I'm not mistaken, Adam and Eve believed in God."

Brenda has been glancing around at the bookstore's shelves. Now she comments, "I don't know if I'd want to read one old book for every new one, but I have to admit, there are a lot of good children's books that have . . . well . . . stood the test of time." She looks apologetic at her use of the trite phrase.

Julia says, "I want to clear something up. I said we should have a new religion, but of course it would include elements from the ancient past. You can't just throw out everything. There are ideas that have . . . well, like Brenda says, stood the test."

"How would you decide what to keep and what to throw away?" Damon asks. Julia remains silent. So does the entire group until Lenae announces, "I'd sure like to see a real dinosaur!"

"Here I am," says Mike.

THE PROBLEM OF EVIL

How Can I Believe in God
When There Is So Much Evil,
Pain and Suffering in the World?

L et's get into a subject that's even more controversial than chronological
snobbery," John says to the group. "In his quest to figure out whether there
is a God, Lewis kept coming up against an obstacle that stops a lot of people: If God exists, why is there so much evil, pain and suffering in this
world? Isn't that inconsistent with an all-good, all-powerful God?"

"Good question." That comment comes from Simon.

Lenae asks, "So what's the answer?"

"Easy. There's no God. Evil is the way the world is. We have to make
whatever good we can out of it."

Julia rushes to break in. "No, no, I believe it's all part of the same thing.
What we call evil, and what we call good, are actually part of the whole,
which means they're ultimately the same thing."

Brenda looks startled. "Are you saying that God is evil?"

"Well, no, but our problem is a matter of perspective. We can't see the whole. If we could only see everything at once, we'd see that there's no distinction between good and evil."

With his usual dry but direct manner, Mike asks, "Where are you going to stand in order to see everything at once?"

Damon, who has been fidgeting in his chair, says, "Let's get back to the basic question. Why is there so much pain in the world? Listen, that's what I asked God when my parents were killed in that car accident. Well, at age ten I didn't care about the world, just about me. But think of all the kids who experience what I experienced, maybe even worse. Why?"

Damon's question hangs in the air. John lets it stay there for a moment before he says, "Lewis struggled with that question too. For him, evil was both an intellectual and an emotional problem. He dealt with the intellectual problem in The Problem of Pain, and with his own emotional struggles in A Grief Observed."

"So, did he solve both problems?" Lenae asks hopefully.

"He reached an intellectual solution, but of course just because you find a solution to the intellectual problem, that doesn't mean you're immune from doubt when you go through painful life experiences."

"So evil made him doubt the existence of God," Brenda suggests.

"Well, this may sound strange, but Lewis came to believe that the existence of evil is actually an argument for God's existence."

The faces of the group go blank, except for Simon, who looks skeptical. Lenae says, "I don't get it."

"Let's talk about it," John says.

THE PROBLEM WE ALL KNOW ABOUT

The problem of evil was perhaps the greatest of all obstacles that stood between C. S. Lewis and the Christian faith. When Lewis met Christians, he would pose the problem to them. He always felt that their efforts to answer were nothing but attempts to avoid the question.

Of course the problem of evil is not unique to Christianity. Every worldview or philosophy has to deal with why suffering exists. In atheism, Hinduism and Buddhism there is no clear basis to call anything evil. We instinctively know better. G. K. Chesterton called original sin "the only doctrine of Christianity that can be empirically proven."

Although we all experience evil, we are cynical about most attempts to explain it. Books and articles on pain and suffering produce immediate skepticism toward the writers. Lewis was aware of the risk: "All arguments in justification of suffering provoke bitter resentment against the author. You would like to know how I behave when I am experiencing pain, not writing books about it."[1] Nevertheless, Lewis did not dodge the issue, and neither can we.

Once when I was asked to speak at a series of seminars on C. S. Lewis, I submitted possible topics for the host's choice. Among the topics were "The Importance of Imagination" and "The Problem of Evil." When I received the publicity for the lecture series, my talk was titled "The Importance of Evil." While I could have corrected the jumbling of words, the error made me think. I decided to talk on the importance of evil from C. S. Lewis's perspective.

A good world gone wrong. As Lewis struggled with the seeming contradiction between an evil world and a good God, he came to see that his own argument depended on the idea that there was, in fact, real evil in the world. Evil was not an illusion or merely a feeling or emotive response to an unpleasant event.

But where had he gotten the concept of evil? His atheism provided no basis for it. Lewis could have said that his idea of evil was just his own private affair, but then his argument against God would collapse too.

If evil was real, then there must be an absolute standard by which it was known to be evil. There must be an absolute good by which evil can be distinguished from good. Where could he find this infinite reference point, this fixed point above all personal and cultural bias? Didn't it demand a God as an adequate basis for absolute good?

As Lewis thought further, he noticed that other worldviews encompassed evil as merely another part of life. In atheism or naturalism (nature is all there is), "evil" is only pain in a world of pain. In Eastern religious perspectives, the view that all is One (pantheism) holds that all distinctions are illusory. Even the distinction between good and evil is part of the illusion.

Yet do we not feel that there are many things in this world that ought not to be the way they are? As Lewis came to believe, our experience tells us that this is a good world gone wrong.

Among many things said about evil, Lewis pointed out that he could argue for the Christian worldview from two phenomena: humor and a horror over dead bodies.[2] I think he meant that both show us that certain things ought not to be as they are.

The argument from humor. One type of humor depends on surprise, like playing peek-a-boo with a baby. A great deal of humor, however, is dependent on a mild unpleasantness—but only a mild unpleasantness because when unpleasantness is too great, when it becomes revolting, then it ceases to be funny. Careers in politics and in the media have been lost because people crossed the line from kidding to outright offensiveness, and it wasn't enough to back up and say "I was only joking."

Humor points to something in life that ought not to be that way. For instance, Rodney Dangerfield made a living predominantly from his one line, "I don't get no respect!" We all know what it is to be taken lightly or to be disrespected, and we all know it ought not to be that way. Humor playfully exposes the difference between *is* and *ought*, between reality as it is and reality as it should be.

The fact that we can legitimately make this distinction points back to a good world where such indignities were not present. It gives us hope for a future where such a distinction is not necessary, where, for instance, people are treated with the respect they deserve.

The argument from horror at death. C. S. Lewis had a particular fear of dead bodies, cemeteries and encounters with things that had died. The horror that we experience in the presence of dead bodies is difficult to erase. Many horror films create fear through images of the living dead, zombies or people crawling out of the grave.

Why do we have a horror of the natural process of death? Could it be that it ought not to be this way? Lewis said that when his friend Charles Williams died, it forever changed his view of death. Was such a vibrant personality lost forever? It ought not be this way!

For three summers I worked in a geriatrics hospital where I had many duties: making beds, shaving patients, giving baths and cleaning. The strangest duty was wrapping the body of a person who had just died, taking it to the hospital morgue, putting it onto a tray, sliding the body into the refrigerated unit and closing the door. Some of the aides used to joke as they wrapped the body, but their humor always seemed forced. It was especially strange to wrap the body of someone you had gotten to know well.

If death is merely part of the natural process—simply the other end of life—then why does it horrify us? Lewis argued that death is unnatural, and its unnaturalness is the source of its horror. Death is an interloper, an intruder on God's good creation, caused by sin. Death ought not to be. It is a clue that this is a good world gone wrong.

THE INTELLECTUAL PROBLEM

Lewis made the existence of evil into an argument for God's existence. But couldn't you turn it around and make the problem of evil into an internal contradiction within theism?

Perhaps philosopher Alvin Plantinga's observation about evil can bring clarity to Lewis's argument. He has shown that the existence of evil in theism cannot be charged to be a necessary contradiction. In summary, the argument goes as follows:

> The all-powerful, all-good God created the universe.
>
> God has permitted evil and has a good reason for doing so.
>
> Therefore, there is no contradiction in theism.[3]

Christianity does not say "God is all-powerful" *and* "God is not all-powerful," or "God is good" *and* "God is not good." If God has permitted evil and "has a good reason for doing so," then there is no necessary contradiction.[4]

Plantinga cautions against any attempt to provide God's reasons for permitting evil. We are unwise if we pretend to be God or even to fully understand him. Yet because we all face pain in some form, we feel compelled to at least try to find some reasons for it. In *The Problem of Pain*, Lewis sets forth the classic lines of explanation for evil. They are free will, natural law and soul making.

Free will. Early in *The Problem of Pain*, Lewis writes, "That we used our free wills to become very bad is so well known that it hardly needs to be stated."[5] Although various Christian traditions hold different views of the meaning of "free will," Christians everywhere appeal to free will as the avenue through which sin came into the world. For example, in the Westminster Confession the answer as to how sin entered the world is "man by the freedom of his will sinned." God did not create evil, but he did create within human beings the capacity to choose evil. While the capacity to choose evil is not evil itself, it provides the possibility for evil to be chosen.

God could have created a world in which evil choices could not be made, but as many believers have argued, such a world would not be the best world.[6]

Natural law. Lewis also argues that in order for our choices to have real consequences we must make those choices in a stable and predictable natural environment.

> As soon as we attempt to introduce the mutual knowledge of fellow-creatures we run up against the necessity of "Nature." People often talk as if nothing were easier than for two naked minds to meet or become aware of each other. But I can see no possibility of their doing so except in a common medium which forms their "external world" or environment.[7]

God could constantly intervene so that no evil consequences ever follow from evil choices, but that would erase the possibility of character formation. Lewis surmises that God could arrange the world so that "a wooden beam became soft as grass when it was used as a weapon, and the air refused to obey me if I attempted to set up in it the sound waves that carry lies or insults. But such a world would be one in which wrong actions were impossible, and in which, therefore, freedom of the will would be void."[8]

Another writer, F. R. Tennant, made a similar observation:

> It cannot be too strongly insisted that a world which is to be a moral order must be a physical order characterized by law and regularity. The theist is only concerned to invoke the fact that law abidingness is an essential condition of the world being a theater of moral life. Without such regularity in physical phenomenon, there could be no probability to guide us: no prediction, no prudence, no accumulation of ordered experience, no

pursuit of premeditated ends, no formation of habit, no possibility of character or culture. Our intellectual faculties could not have been developed . . . and without rationality, morality is impossible.[9]

God could turn wooden beams into grass, turn bullets into marshmallows and thus eliminate evil consequences, but what would that do to the seriousness of moral choices?

But couldn't God have created another kind of nature where things do not have the capacity to hurt us? Such a world is difficult to imagine. In our world all good things have a potential for evil use or harm. Fire can be used for light, for cooking and for warmth, but it can also burn our bodies or possessions. Lewis points out that "fire comforts that body at a certain distance; it will destroy it when the distance is reduced "[10] Water can be used for drinking, swimming, boating or water-skiing; but it can also drown a person. Wood could be used, Lewis says, as a building beam or to hit a neighbor on the head. The same nature that can cause pain can cause pleasure. Our sexuality can bring great pleasure or cause great physical and emotional pain. Evil twists God's divinely intended uses of good creation into abuses that cause pain. In *The Screwtape Letters* Lewis has a demon describe God:

> He's a hedonist at heart. . . . He makes no secret of it; at His right hand are "pleasures forevermore." . . . He's vulgar, Wormwood. He has a bourgeois mind. He has filled His world full of pleasures. There are things for humans to do all day long . . . sleeping, washing, eating, drinking, making love, playing, praying, working. Everything has to be twisted before it's any use to us.[11]

Soul making. Lewis maintained that we live in the "vale of soul-making" where we are offered critical choices about how to respond to evil, and our choices have far-reaching consequences.[12] Pain presents us with an opportunity for victory or defeat. We must choose how we will face suffering: let it overcome us or rise above it. In his book *Creative Suffering*, Paul Tournier argues that all great human leaders have had to overcome painful experiences in order to rise to leadership.

Above all, pain wakes us up and makes us ask fundamental questions that we might not ask otherwise. Lewis writes in *The Problem of Pain:* "Pain insists on being attended to. God whispers to us in our pleasures, speaks in our conscience, but shouts in our pains: it is His megaphone to rouse a deaf world. . . . It plants the flag of truth within the fortress of a rebel soul."[13]

Pain not only gets our attention; it also shatters the illusion that things can satisfy us. Apart from pain, it is easy to let ourselves be distracted from what is most important in life. Lewis quotes Augustine: "God wants to give us something but cannot because our hands are full—there's nowhere for Him to put it."[14]

Odd as it sounds, pain aids our ability to seek God. When we experience even relatively minor pain, say that of a toothache, we cannot attend to much else until we get relief. And of course many types of pain are far greater than a toothache. When we are in the depths of despair and agony, we cry out to God in a way that we seldom—perhaps never—do otherwise.

Pain and suffering are also the soil in which heroism and acts of great benevolence flower. The events surrounding September 11, 2001, saw not only police and firefighters but also ordinary citizens give their lives or work to alleviate the pain of others. But we must acknowledge that pain can also crush someone to the point of despair. Suffering brings the possibility of real gain or real loss.

We may never get an answer. Though we may be persuaded that free will, natural law and soul making give us some glimpse into why pain exists, that insight does not solve our struggle with evil once and for all. Intellectual answers can never give specific reasons for why God permits the particular evils we encounter. In the Bible, Job never receives an explanation for his sufferings. Instead, after a long silence, God asks a series of questions that show Job the limitations of his own understanding. Job learns to trust in God, who alone knows why. Charles Williams, Lewis's close friend and fellow Inkling, once reminded Lewis that the weight of God's displeasure was reserved for Job's comforters who tried to show that all was well: "The sort of people, Williams said, who wrote books on the problem of pain."[15]

LEWIS'S EMOTIONAL STRUGGLE

Lewis could write masterfully about suffering, but faced with the prospect of real suffering in his own life, he was acutely aware of the gulf between theory and practice. In his introduction to *The Problem of Pain* he wrote:

> I have never for one moment been in a state of mind to which even the imagination of serious pain was less than intolerable. If any man is safe from the danger of underestimating this adversary, I am that man. I must add too, that the only purpose of the book is to solve the intellectual problem raised by suffering; for the far higher task of teaching fortitude and patience I was never a fool enough to suppose myself qualified.[16]

C. S. Lewis's intellectual answers to the problem of pain were tested to the breaking point by the illness and death of his wife, Joy.

The unusual circumstances of Jack and Joy's marriage are powerfully portrayed in the BBC and Hollywood movie versions of *Shadow-*

lands. Joy and Jack were married in a civil ceremony in 1956, and later, when Joy was diagnosed with cancer, they were married by an Anglican priest in 1957. Shortly after this second ceremony, Joy had a remission of her cancer. She was able to progress from bed to wheelchair to almost normal walking with the aid of a cane. The next couple of years were filled with remarkable happiness. Joy wrote in mid-1957: "Jack and I are managing to be surprisingly happy, considering the circumstances; you would think we were a honeymoon couple in our early twenties rather than our middle-aged selves."[17]

C. S. Lewis commented that he experienced later in life the married bliss that most people experience in their early years. However, it did not last. By late 1959 the cancer returned, and Joy died on July 13, 1960. Two of the last things she said were, "You have made me happy," and "I am at peace with God."[18]

A grief observed. The loss of Joy plunged Jack into the depths of grief and pain. Following her death, Lewis kept a journal and wrote down his thoughts with no intent of publication. Later he published his journal under the pseudonym N. W. Clerk (a pun on the Old English for "I know not what scholar"). Titled *A Grief Observed,* it was published two years before Lewis's own death. Ironically, when the book first came out, many people thought it would be helpful to Jack, and he received gift copies.

A Grief Observed reveals the process through which Lewis dealt with and began to emerge from his grief. The path was much clouded by fear, doubt and anger before the gradual lifting of the darkness and the breaking through of the sun.

Lewis experienced a devastating sense of distance from God, what the sixteenth-century monk John of the Cross called the "dark night of the soul." Lewis wrote: "But go to Him when your need is desperate, when all other help is vain, and what do you find? A door slammed in your face, and a sound of bolting and double bolting on the inside. After that, silence."[19]

Not only did God seem distant, but Lewis began to doubt that God was good after all. The danger was not that Lewis would become an atheist. Instead, he wrote: "The real danger is of coming to believe such dreadful things about Him. The conclusion I dread is not, 'So there's no God after all,' but, 'So this is what God's really like. Deceive yourself no longer.' "[20]

Anger at God. I remember my first reading of *A Grief Observed*. When I came across some of the early passages where Lewis expresses awful thoughts about God, they were too much for me. I stopped reading. I am glad I later picked up the book again and continued to the end. Lewis came to realize that his delight in such vicious thoughts revealed his anger at God and a desire to get back at him:

> In a way I liked them. I am even aware of a slight reluctance to accept the opposite thoughts. All that stuff about the Cosmic Sadist was not so much the expression of thought as of hatred. I was getting from it the only pleasure a man in anguish can get; the pleasure of hitting back. . . . "[T]elling God what I thought of Him." And of course, as in all abusive language, "what I thought" didn't mean what I thought true. Only what I thought would offend Him (and His worshippers) most. That sort of thing is never said without some pleasure. Gets it "off your chest." You feel better for a moment.[21]

While it is not necessary to experience anger at God in the same way or to the same intensity Lewis did, it is certainly not unusual. Even a cursory look at the Psalms confirms this. I think that in many cases, atheists do not really disbelieve in God; rather, they believe in

him and are angry with him. Their assertion of God's nonexistence
gives them a perverse delight.

Clouds begin to lift. By small degrees some of the clouds of grief
started to lift for Lewis. One of the breakthroughs was his realization
that his desire for Joy to come back to him might not be good for her:

> I never even raised the question whether such a return, if it
> were possible, would be good for her. I want her back as an in-
> gredient in the restoration of my past. Could I have wished her
> anything worse? Having got once through death, to come back
> and then, at some later date, have all her dying to do over again?
> They call Stephen the first martyr. Hadn't Lazarus the rawer
> deal?[22]

Unexpectedly, one day Jack's heart felt lighter. "It came this morning early. . . . [M]y heart was lighter than it had been for many
weeks."[23] Some of the relief he attributed to recovery from physical
exhaustion, due to a few good nights' sleep. Gradually he began to
feel a breakthrough in his relationship with God. The door was no
longer shut and bolted.

> Was it my own frantic need that slammed it in my face? The
> time when there is nothing at all in your soul except a cry for
> help may be just the time when God cannot give it. You are like
> the drowning man who cannot be helped because he clutches
> or grabs. Perhaps your own reiterated cries deafen you to the
> voice you hoped to hear.[24]

There was no abrupt transition from fear, anger, grief and pain to
warmth and light. The change was "like the warming of a room or the
coming of daylight. When you first notice them, they have been already going on for some time."[25] Jack came to see that ultimately

some of his questions were unanswerable even by God:

> When I lay these questions before God I get no answer. But a
> rather special sort of "No answer." It is not the locked door. It
> is more like a silent, certainly not uncompassionate, gaze. As
> though He shook His head not in refusal but waiving the ques-
> tion. Like, "Peace, child; you don't understand." Can a mortal
> ask questions which God finds unanswerable? Quite easily, I
> should think. All nonsense questions are unanswerable. How
> many hours are there in a mile? Is yellow square or round?
> Probably half the questions we ask—half our great theological
> and metaphysical problems—are like that.[26]

Lewis's faith was gradually restored to its robust quality, as we can
see by the end of *A Grief Observed* and in his final book *Letters to Malcolm: Chiefly on Prayer.* He had suffered his worst pain and come out
stronger on the other side.

THE DIVINE WEAVING

Corrie ten Boom, the Dutch Christian who with her family helped
Jews escape Nazi-occupied Holland in WWII, spent ten months in
German prison camps. Of the seven members of her family who were
imprisoned, four died, including Corrie's father and her sister Betsie.
After her release Corrie shared her message that Jesus' love was
greater than all suffering and evil. In her messages she often quoted
the poem "The Weaver":

> My life is but a weaving between my Lord and me.
> I cannot choose the colors, He worketh steadily.
> Oft times he weaveth sorrow, and I in foolish pride,
> Forget He sees the upper, and I the underside.

Not till the looms are silent and the shuttles cease to fly,
Will God unroll the canvas and explain the reason why
The dark threads are as needful in the Weaver's skillful hand
As the threads of gold and silver in the pattern He has planned.
GRANT COLFAX TULLER

In the end all analogies fall short because we still find it impossible to discern any redeeming value in some evils. Lewis observes that when we experience pain, a little courage helps more than much knowledge, a little sympathy more than much courage, and the least amount of the love of God more than all.[27]

So what can we learn from Lewis's approach to the problem of evil?

• Evil is a clue to the cosmos—that this is a good world gone wrong.

• If evil is real, then those worldviews that deny the existence of real evil are false (atheism, Hinduism, Buddhism and neopaganism).

• Lewis's possible explanations for evil include free will, natural law and soul making.

• Even when you come to an intellectual answer for the problem of evil, that answer may not suffice for your emotional suffering. Lewis reveals how he worked through the emotional pain of grief and loss in *A Grief Observed*.

TRUST, NOT PROOF

Frowning a little, Lenae says, "So Lewis kind of came to an answer and kind of didn't. He got mad at God, but he still believed God existed."

"Not only existed, but could be trusted," John adds. "And Lewis learned to trust God even if he didn't understand God completely—which none of us does, by the way."

"I never thought, says Damon, "about the possibility that suffering could

be evidence for God. So Lewis said that we wouldn't have any concept of evil if we didn't also have a concept of good—ultimate good."

"But ultimate good doesn't necessarily mean God," Simon puts in quickly. "Our idea of good could come from within ourselves."

With a very definite tone Julia says, "I agree that suffering makes you seek after God. I went through some difficult experiences in my life and that's what started my spiritual quest."

Brenda almost snorts as she asks, "So God clobbers people in order to get their attention?"

"If we weren't so bull-headed, maybe he wouldn't have to," Mike suggests.

Simon shrugs and says, "Look, we bring these things on ourselves. Bad things happen and we try to explain them by superstition and mythology."

Julia seems glad for the change of subject. "Mythology! I love mythology! John, didn't you say that Lewis was big on mythology? Wait, you said it was one of his obstacles. I hope he didn't throw it all away."

"By no means, Julia. You could say that Lewis's love for mythology was an obstacle that became a gateway to faith. This is where Tolkien comes into the story in a big way."

MYTH

Isn't Christianity
Just One Myth Among Many?

J ulia says, *"I'm a fan of Joseph Campbell. He says that all religion is myth. I think that's a fascinating concept. We invent these myths to explain the world. They can sustain whole societies."*

"What exactly do you mean when you say 'myth'?" Lenae asks. "You mean like the ancient Greek gods, like Zeus and—who's another one— Hercules?"

John explains, "C. S. Lewis defined myth as an 'unfocused gleam of divine truth falling on human imagination.'[1] But that was after his conversion. From an early age, he was fascinated by mythology, particularly Norse mythology."

"So what was the problem?" Brenda asks. "Myths are great stories. Why would they set up some kind of obstacle to believing in God or . . . or Christ?" She seems reluctant to say the final word.

Mike suggests, "I think I can see why. If all those other stories of gods are just myth, why wouldn't the Bible be myth too?"

"The Bible is a collection of folk tales," Simon tells the group with great authority. "If you want to call them myth, OK. Same thing, basically."

John says, "I'm going to surprise you. At one point Lewis's view was similar to Joseph Campbell's, not that Campbell was around then of course. In his process of becoming a Christian, he had to come around to the idea that myths are not false but true."

Damon says "Huh?" and the word is written on everyone else's face.

EXEMPT FROM CRITICISM?

In *Surprised by Joy*, Lewis wrote that one factor that contributed to his atheism was the similarity between Christianity and pagan mythology. In his secondary education it was assumed that pagan myths were false and Christianity true. He wondered on what basis Christianity should be exempt from the same critical judgment that was passed on myths. He says:

> No one ever attempted to show in what sense Christianity fulfilled Paganism or Paganism prefigured Christianity. The accepted position seemed to be that religions were normally a mere farrago of nonsense, though our own, by a fortunate exception, was exactly true. . . . But on what grounds could I believe in this exception? It obviously was in some general sense the same kind of thing as all the rest. Why was it so differently treated? Need I, at any rate, continue to treat it differently? I was very anxious not to.[2]

Lewis was particularly drawn to Norse mythology. Once as a young man he saw an illustration from "Siegfried and the Twilight of the Gods." Even this little observation was enough to kindle immense emotion. He recalled, "Pure 'Northerness' engulfed me: a vision of huge, clear spaces hanging above the Atlantic in the endless twilight of the Northern summer, remoteness, severity. . . . [T]he memory of Joy itself."[3] This mythic consciousness continued throughout his life.

Lewis's ongoing study in preparation for Oxford continued to reinforce his doubts. When he was studying with Kirkpatrick in 1916, he wrote to friend Arthur Greeves: "You ask me my religious views: you know, I think that I believe in no religion. There is absolutely no proof for any of them, and from a philosophical standpoint Christianity is not even the best. All religions, that is, all mythologies to give them their proper name, are merely man's invention."[4] After giving a Freudian type of explanation for the origin of religions, Lewis continues his letter:

> Often too, great men were regarded as gods after their death— such as Heracles or Odin: thus after the death of a Hebrew philosopher Yeshua (whose name we have corrupted into Jesus) he became regarded as a god, a cult sprang up, which was afterward connected with the ancient Hebrew Jahweh-worship, and so Christianity came into being—one mythology among many, but one that we happened to be brought up in."[5]

PAGAN AMONG PURITANS

Lewis was so captivated by myth that he called himself "a converted Pagan living among apostate Puritans."[6] It was in such a state of mind—regarding Christianity as one myth among many—that Lewis went to Oxford and later was given a position on the faculty.

Lewis first met J. R. R. Tolkien (author of *Lord of the Rings*) at an Oxford faculty meeting, May 11, 1926. Lewis wrote in his diary about Tolkien that he was "a smooth, pale, fluent little chap. . . . No harm in him; only needs a smack or so."[7] The relationship developed, and in 1927 Tolkien, finding a fellow lover of myths, invited Lewis to join the Coalbiters Club, which focused on reading Icelandic mythology. These and other regular meetings allowed Tolkien (a Christian) and Lewis (at this time an atheist) to talk about issues of faith.

Are myths lies? One night Lewis, Tolkien and Hugo Dyson were having dinner at Magdalen College. Lewis expressed his difficulty with the parallels between pagan mythology and the Gospels. Lewis said that "myths are lies." Tolkien responded forcefully, "No they are not." This led to a discussion lasting almost all night, during which they walked around Oxford and talked through this issue.

Myths in Tolkien's view, although they may contain errors, also reflect part of God's reality. God has created the world and the human mind. Within that structure of divine reality it is not surprising that similar stories would emerge. Myths are splintered fragments of the true light. Becoming a "sub-creator"—inventing myths—is something central to our humanity. Tolkien later wrote in a letter: "I believe that legends and myths are largely made of truth, and indeed present aspects of it can only be perceived in this mode; and long ago certain truths and modes of this kind were discovered and must always appear."[8]

The good catastrophe. I have heard that there are only eight basic stories and all the others are just variations and combinations of these basic core stories. One of the common elements to a good story is what Tolkien called a "eucatastrophe," a good catastrophe. This is a tragedy in the midst of the story that ends up being a good thing, leading to the "happily ever after" at the end.

For example, in Snow White, the heroine's eating from the poisoned apple and seeming to die only provides the opportunity for the kiss from her Prince Charming. They then live happily ever after in their castle in the clouds. Without the catastrophe, there is no happy ending. Many stories contain this element. In fact, Tolkien argued that the mark of a good fairy story is this "eucatastrophe" leading to the happy ending.

This happy ending, far from being naive and unrealistic, denies that the universe will end in final defeat. The happy ending is "evangelium [good news], giving a fleeting glimpse of Joy, Joy beyond the walls of the world, poignant as grief."[9] Tolkien goes on to argue in the epilogue of his classic essay "On Fairy Stories" that the gospel of Christ is the greatest "eucatastrophe" of history. The worst has already happened—the Son of God died on a cross. But of course that was not the end of the story. The crucifixion led to the resurrection: great joy and victory over death. Tolkien says: "The Birth of Christ is the eucatastrophe of Man's history. The Resurrection is the eucatastrophe of the story of the Incarnation. This history begins and ends in joy. . . . There is no tale ever told that men would rather find was true."[10]

True myth. We do not know all the content of the late night conversation between Lewis and Tolkien, but it probably went along the lines given above. Tolkien also argued that the gospel is not just a nice story; it is fact. The gospel of Christ was a "myth become fact." The difference between Christ and pagan mythology was that the Gospels were historically true and not just fiction.

When Lewis examined the Gospel narratives, having already become an expert in mythology, he was surprised to find that his literary judgment told him that they were more than myths:

> I was by now too experienced in literary criticism to regard the
> Gospels as myths. They had not the mythical taste. And yet the
> very matter that they set down in their artless, historical fashion

. . . was precisely the matter of the great myths. If ever a myth had become fact, had been incarnated, it would be just like this. . . . Here and here only in all time the myth must have become fact; the Word, flesh; God, Man.[11]

Not long after the late night discussion with Tolkien and Dyson, Lewis came to believe that Christ was the Son of God. He wrote to Arthur Greeves saying that the discussion with Tolkien and Dyson had influenced him to believe that "the story of Christ is simply a true myth: a myth working on us in the same way as others, but with this tremendous difference that it really happened."[12]

Pagan myths, what Lewis sometimes called "good dreams," are found in many places. Characters such as Adonis, Balder, Bacchus, Osiris and others emerge. Sometimes these "gods" die and rise again. Lewis says, "From a certain point of view Christ is the same sort of thing as Adonis or Osiris."[13] Yet Christ is the only one of these who might be historical. Perhaps if Plato or the myth-makers were to have heard about Christ, they would have said, "I see, . . . so that is what I was really talking about."

LEWIS ON BIBLICAL CRITICISM

Of course, there are theologians who insist that the Bible contains much that is mythical. The miracle stories in particular are regarded as "myth," meaning in this case unhistorical or fictional. In effect, this means that much of the character and personality of Jesus was invented. Jesus did not create the narrative; the narrative (written by some early individuals) created Jesus.

In Lewis's day the scholars who maintained this view were Paul Tillich and, most prominently, Rudolf Bultmann. Today this view continues to be advocated by the Jesus Seminar and assorted others.

It has become the liberal theological orthodoxy: for someone of this persuasion to question this theory is to lose credibility and respect in their community of scholars.

For about ten years I attended such a seminary while doing my master of divinity and Ph.D. I remember one such professor telling me he did not read a book that did not assume this radical criticism. This view was put forward as the only responsible intellectual option, and all other views were ridiculed. Not once did I hear a professor expound a more conservative view and then provide a critique of it. It was as if such conservative alternatives did not exist except to be rejected out of hand as not worthy of attention.

Once C. S. Lewis was meeting with Bishop Kenneth Carey, then principal of Westcott House, the theological college based in Cambridge. While the bishop was out of the room, Lewis picked up a book and read Alec Vidler's sermon "The Sign at Cana." When the bishop came back, he asked Lewis what he thought about the sermon. Candidly, Lewis said that it was incredible to have to wait two-thousand years to be told that this miracle (turning water into wine) was really a parable. Lewis's comment led to a further discussion where Lewis told Carey what he thought about such criticism. This led to a request that Lewis talk about the subject to some theological students. Lewis's talk, "Modern Theology and Biblical Criticism," is found in the book *Christian Reflections*, a collection of his writings.

Lewis began his talk by saying that he was not professionally educated as a theologian, but neither was he uneducated. He was educated in another discipline that happened to be relevant to the biblical criticism that had been going on for a couple of hundred years. He was an expert in literary criticism and both by inclination and profession a student of mythology. He said that it might be worth hearing what a sheep could tell the shepherds, and he proceeds with what he calls "my bleating."[14]

Lewis argues that he distrusts these biblical critics as literary critics. Perhaps their study of the New Testament qualifies them as professionals in that area, but what qualifies them as literary critics? It would be good to know, when they call a biblical story a myth or a legend, how many myths and legends they have read. Often, for instance (Lewis quotes one author), the Gospel of John is regarded as a romance, a poem or a parable like *Pilgrim's Progress*. Now *Pilgrim's Progress* is clearly an allegory, with everything having symbolic meaning. But looking at the Gospel of John where Jesus dialogues with the Samaritan woman (chap. 4) or the healing of the man born blind (chap. 9), Lewis says: "I have been reading poems, romances, vision literature, legends, and myths all my life. I know what they are like. I know that not one of them is like this."[15] Either the biblical author is telling us something considered factually true, or else the author has precociously anticipated the modern fiction novel and is writing fiction in a realistic way.

After some other examples, Lewis considers a quote by Bultmann to the effect that "the personality of Jesus has no importance for the kerygma [preaching] of Paul or of John." Lewis comments, "Through what strange process has this learned German gone in order to make himself blind to what all men except him see? . . . If anything whatever is common to all believers, and even to many unbelievers, it is the sense that in the Gospels they have met a personality."[16]

Lewis's main problem with this kind of criticism is that it claims that it can read between the lines of old texts. Lewis questions whether they can even "read . . . the lines themselves. They claim to see fern-seed and can't see an elephant ten yards away in broad daylight."[17]

JESUS MISREMEMBERED?

A second "bleat" that Lewis makes is that this modern view claims that the real purpose and teaching of Christ was soon forgotten, misunderstood or misrepresented by the early church, but now it has been discovered by modern scholars. Lewis was familiar with the phenomenon in literature. Concerning Shakespearian studies he says, "Every week a clever undergraduate, every quarter a dull American don discovers for the first time what some Shakespearian play really meant."[18] Often the reinterpretation reflects a mindset common to contemporary thinking but foreign to Shakespeare's day. In the same way, the "Jesus" discovered by the various quests for the historical Jesus tends to be a reflection of the modern author's personality and philosophical stance.

The form critics imagine a free-flowing situation in the first and second century that allowed and even encouraged the easy invention of stories about Jesus. However, such a picture is totally contrary to the Middle Eastern and Jewish environment out of which these stories come. In the book *Memory and Manuscript* Birger Gerhardsson thoroughly documents the importance of memorization for the Jewish mentality.

The good Jewish student was not to lose a drop from the cistern of the master's teaching. To this day the best Jewish student is the one who can recite the rabbinic tradition verbatim on issue after issue. (For a contemporary novel illustrating this phenomenon, read *The Chosen* by Chaim Potok.) No one was encouraged to play fast and loose with the formal tradition. You were not allowed creative freedom. You must recite word for word; you would be immediately corrected if a single word was wrong.

Such feats of memory continue in the Middle East today. Kenneth

Bailey lived in the Middle East for sixty years and for part of that time taught at a University in Beirut, Lebanon. He points out that memory is still vital in Middle Eastern culture. Even the illiterate peasant knows thousands of proverbs and lines of poetry by heart. A game that is sometimes played has a large number of participants sit in a circle. The game begins when the first person recites two lines of po etry. The next person has to use the last letter of the last line as the first letter of two other lines of poetry, and so on. Bailey reports that he has seen the game played many times, even by those who cannot read, where the game travels several cycles around the circle (of ten to fifteen people) before anyone is stumped or mistaken in quotation. Everybody knows when you make a mistake, and you have to sit out.[19]

Some youth leaders tried to bring the American game of "telephone" to the Middle East, but it did not work. In this game a short message is given to the first person, who then whispers that message into the next person's ear and so on around the circle. The results are often funny because the message comes out garbled at the other end. In the Middle East, however, the message came back exactly the same. The Middle Eastern kids could not see the fun in the game, since they were trained to hear carefully and repeat exactly.

Many Muslims are encouraged to memorize the Qur'an in Arabic. A translation or a paraphrase will not do. It has to be an exact repetition of the Arabic. One of the terrorists from September 11, 2001, was said to have memorized the whole Qur'an. Biblical scholar Bruce Waltke said that he once met a man in Israel who had memorized the whole Old Testament in Hebrew. Waltke tested the man on his knowledge and found his claim to be true. However, Waltke was surprised to learn that the man was an atheist.

Not only are the Qur'an, the Old Testament and cultural poetry and proverbs memorized carefully, but informal tradition or stories are given the same care. Bailey gave an illustration of a book written about a century ago about the founding of a Christian church in a Middle Eastern community. When he went to visit that community and asked about the founding of the church, the stories he was told matched those in the book, even down to the quotations. The remarkable accuracy was not because the people had read the book, but because the tradition has been passed on with scrupulous care.[20]

If the formal tradition of a teacher is passed on verbatim and the informal stories, especially about the founding of community life, are passed on with extreme care, then how do we account for the invention of fictional stories about a person named Jesus being passed off as true, with no protest, shock, and outrage expressed? It might have happened in some other time and place, but not in Israel or in the Middle East. Jesus died around A.D. 30. The Gospel of Mark was written in the 60s if not in the 50s. Paul received his tradition in the mid-30s and also wrote in the early 50s. Where is there the time for the creation of legends and myths? The development of German folklore required centuries. Yet the message of the gospel exploded into life fully grown at birth.[21] The evidence is that the people of the first century meticulously preserved the exact words and accurately passed on the stories about their founder Jesus.

If critical scholars would listen to Lewis's advice and interpret biblical stories in light of first-century Jewish assumptions rather than imposing their contemporary bias and beliefs on the text, many of their own doubts could be addressed.

CAN GOD INTERVENE?

Third, Lewis questions the critics' assumptions that miracles just do not happen. If the Gospels record a prophetic prediction by Jesus, the critics assume that it was put into his mouth by later writers after the prophecy was fulfilled. Why? Because (the critics assume) prophetic prediction of events cannot occur before they happen.

Similarly, any miracles recorded in the Gospels are regarded as un-historical. Why? Because, according to the critics, miracles cannot happen. It has always amazed me that many of these theological crit-ics, though they do not claim to be atheists and believe in some kind of God, allow no possibility for God to intervene in creation. Their assumption—"if miraculous, then unhistorical"—does not come out of the text but is brought to it. A miracle story is judged a "myth" not because it has the form, taste and literary trappings of myth but be-cause it is assumed that it has to be fiction. Lewis says: "If one is speaking of authority, the united authority of all the Biblical critics in the world counts here for nothing. On this they speak simply as men, men obviously influenced by, and perhaps insufficiently critical of, the spirit of the age they grew up in,"[22] They are in captivity to mod-ernism—the whole rationalistic spirit of the Enlightenment.[23]

Lewis's fourth "bleat," his loudest and longest, is that the attempt to reconstruct the origin of texts (when, where, for what purpose they were written) ought to be regarded with great skepticism. Many people attempted to reconstruct C. S. Lewis's process in writing. Of these "imaginary histories," "not one of these guesses has on any one point been right: . . . the method shows a record of 100 percent fail-ure."[24]

Another illustration Lewis gives of such misjudgment by critics is Tolkien's *Lord of the Rings*. Many reviewers connected the ring in the story with the atomic bomb. Yet the "chronology of the book's com-position makes it impossible."[25]

When people have attempted to reconstruct an ancient text, "the results are either always, or else nearly always wrong." If results about contemporary writers, writing the same language and context as ours, are so abysmal, what hope can we place in the "assured results of modern scholarship" about events two thousand years ago in a different language and radically different cultural context?

I remember sitting in Ph.D. colloquiums where very impressive papers were presented by evangelicals who critiqued the foundational principles of the critical methods. I observed a wide difference between the responses of liberal Ph.D. students and liberal professors. In many cases the students agreed with the critiques or at least acknowledged their forcefulness and wondered aloud whether such theories should be scrapped. On the other hand, the professors were adamantly opposed, not because they had an answer for the criticisms but because they had no alternative theories to put in their place.

THE RIGHT KIND OF SKEPTICISM

Lewis's role in his talk was not so much to eliminate skepticism as to encourage it. He wanted to encourage doubt about the "whole demythology of our time."[26] Lewis wrote in *Letters to Malcolm,* "By the way, did you ever meet, or hear of anyone who was converted from skepticism to a liberal or demythologized Christianity? I think that when unbelievers come in at all, they come in a good deal further."[27]

It is not often that sheep speak so frankly with shepherds. Lewis asked his hearers to listen to his "bleating" because "you will not perhaps hear them very often again. Your parishioners will not often speak to you quite frankly." It is embarrassing to be a missionary to the priests of the church, but if such mission work is not done "the future history of the Church of England is likely to be short."[28]

So to the charge that Christianity is only one myth among many, Lewis would say:

- Myths are not outright lies. They contain truth. Given the structure of the human mind and the structure of God's creation, we should not be surprised that there are similarities among myths.

- We must ask, "Are any of the myths truer than any of the others?" or more precisely, "Are any of these myths also fact?" Christ is *the* myth become fact.

- It is surprising to see so many shepherds of the church who believe that the Gospels are largely mythical. They may have some expertise in the Bible, but there remains a serious question about whether they are experts in literature and mythology.

- We do not have to reject all the knowledge gained by critics' study in order to be skeptical of some of their "assured results."

TRUE MYTH

As usual, Brenda voices a strong opinion. "So why does any myth have to be true? Why did that matter so much to Lewis? Myths are great stories. All children love them, and so do adults. Who cares if they really happened?"

John ponders a moment. He expects Simon to jump in and fill the silence, but the only sound is the murmur of customers' voices in the bookstore. In the little circle in the corner, there is quiet. Finally John ventures, "I guess no myth has to be true. But suppose one was true? Do you agree with what Tolkien said about the story of Christ? That there is no other myth that we would rather find out was true?"

"I wouldn't be so sure," says Simon thoughtfully.

Julia asks him, "You mean you'd rather it wasn't true?"

"Well, let's just say if it was . . ." He does not finish his sentence.

John says to the group as a whole, "If Christianity is true, if Jesus Christ really is who he says he is, then it changes everything. At least that's what

I think. What do all of you think?"

"I guess if he's real, then we'd better pay more attention to him," says Lenae. "I mean, pay attention to what he said, his commands, that kind of thing."

"I'm realizing," Damon admits, "I don't know much about all that. I grew up in foster homes where we didn't go to church, and I've never read the Bible much."

Mike gestures toward the bookstore shelves and says, "Good place to start. You'll find them in any size or color you want here."

Brenda interrupts, "But we don't need a myth to tell us how to live. We're all reasonable people here, right? We can figure out for ourselves what to do and what's right and wrong for us."

John nods and says, "That's exactly what C. S. Lewis's early teachers taught him—that reason is all we need."

"I need a break," Mike says. "How about if we wait till next week to get reasonable?"

Rationalism

Who Needs Faith?

When the group has gathered for their third meeting, John directs a question to Lenae. "Lenae, didn't you tell us you came here because you wanted to think more about your faith?"

"Well, I wouldn't say I wanted to, but this friend of mine is always telling me I should. She's what you'd call a deep thinker."

Brenda, half kidding and half serious, asks "So is this group helping you think deeper?"

"Yeah, in a way. I'm hearing about things I never thought of before. I get the idea that if C. S. Lewis were here, he'd make us think, whether we wanted to or not."

John explains, "In Lewis's time, the dominant view of life was what we now call modernism. Modernism placed great confidence in reason, the scientific method and rational arguments. We can also call this view rationalism."

Simon speaks up. "I'd call myself a rationalist. I'm convinced that all the evidence points to the conclusion that it is not reasonable to believe in the supernatural, including a supreme being."

Julia protests, "But belief isn't a matter of reason, it's a matter of the life experiences that are sent to you on your spiritual path."

Damon points out, "Yeah, but Lewis came to believe in God, and he was sure reasonable." Then he looks thoughtful. "Or did Lewis eventually abandon his reason, the more he got into Christianity?"

"Hardly," John says. "He remained a tough thinker. But he did come to reject hard-core modernism."

Lenae says, "So postmodernism must be what came after modernism, right? My friend—the one who's a real thinker—personally I think she thinks too much—anyway, one time I said we can't know anything about God for sure, I mean absolutely for certain. And she said I was a good example of postmodernism. I don't think she meant it as a compliment."

"Hold on, can we define some terms here?" Mike asks. "I'm getting confused with all these isms." Around the circle several people nod in agreement.

John holds up a small dry-erase board. Simon groans and says, "Here comes the Sunday school lesson," but he says it good-naturedly. John grins at him and explains, "There are four basic intellectual positions about the relationship between faith and reason. We can represent them as mathematical equations, where R stands for reason and F stands for faith." John writes:

$R - F = M$ (modernism or rationalism)

$F - R = f$ (fideism or faith-ism)

$- F - R = P$ (postmodernism)

$F + R = C$ (classical approach)

John explains, "Modernism/rationalism (M) placed reason in the supreme place and subtracted faith. Fideism or faith-ism (f) is at the opposite pole. It's faith to the exclusion of reason, where reason is of little or no value in understanding divine things. Some forms of postmodernism eliminate any objective basis for reason or faith. And as you've probably figured out, the classical approach, faith plus reason, is the view Lewis eventually arrived at although he held to this position in a unique way." He chuckles a little to himself as the group members squint at the board. He can tell they're trying to figure out where they fit.

A PLACE FOR REASON

C. S. Lewis definitely saw a place for reason in the Christian faith. He wrote: "I'm not asking anyone to accept Christianity if his best reasoning tells him that the weight of evidence is against it."[1] Lewis believed that there was enough evidence for Christ to lead to the psychological exclusion of doubt, but not the logical exclusion of dispute.

Yet while he maintained a place for reason, Lewis was not a modernist. Remember that he studied under W. T. Kirkpatrick ("Kirk"), who was the epitome of nineteenth-century rationalism. While Kirk greatly assisted Lewis's ability to think clearly, Lewis came to reject Kirk's rationalism.

LEWIS AGAINST PURE RATIONALISM

Lewis wrote his first book in defense of the faith, Pilgrim's Regress, only two years after he came to faith in Christ. The hero, John, sets out from Puritania on a quest for an island that he has seen in a vision. Puritania is a place where people still believe in the Landlord (God). Unlike Pilgrim in Pilgrim's Progress, John does not encounter general temptations on his path to glory. Rather he is met by specific intellectual advocates of the modernist worldview similar to those Lewis faced every day at Oxford. One of the first characters John meets is Mr. Enlightenment.

"And where might you come from my fine lad?" said Mr. Enlightenment.

"From Puritania, sir," said John.

"A good place to leave, eh?"

"I'm so glad you think that," said John.

"I hope I'm a man of this world," said Mr. Enlightenment.
"Any young fellow anxious to better himself may depend on
finding sympathy and support in me. Puritania! Why, I suppose
you have been brought up to be afraid of the Landlord?"

"Well, I must admit I sometimes do feel rather nervous."

"You may make your mind easy, my boy. There is no such
person."

"There is no Landlord?"

"There is absolutely no such thing—I might even say no such
entity—in existence. There never has been and never will be."

"And is this absolutely certain?" cried John, for a great hope
was rising in his heart.

"Absolutely certain. Look at me, young man. I ask you—do
I look as if I was easily taken in?"[2]

A little later John asks, "But how do you KNOW there is no Landlord?"

"Christopher Columbus, Galileo, the earth is round, the invention of printing, gunpowder!" exclaimed Mr. Enlightenment in
such a loud voice that the pony shied.

"I beg your pardon," said John.

"Eh?" said Mr. Enlightenment.

"I didn't quite understand," said John.

When Mr. Enlightenment argues against the truth of many religious
stories, John summarizes his argument:

"I think I see. Most of the stories about the Landlord are probably untrue; therefore, the rest are probably untrue."

"Well that's about as near as a beginner can get to it perhaps. But when you have had scientific training, you will find that you can be quite certain about all sorts of things which now seem to you only probable."

In the final encounter John comments, "I'm not sure that I have really understood your arguments, sir. Is it absolutely certain that there is no Landlord?"

"Absolutely. I give you my word of honour."[4]

Notice how the rationalist covers the deficiency of argument with dogmatic assertions. Notice too how quickly and smoothly he moves from probability to certainty: "you can be quite certain about all sorts of things which now seem to you only probable." The strength of the assertion covers the deficiency of the argument.

DIFFICULTY OF NEGATIVE PROOF

The dogmatic rationalist/modernist tries to assert absolutely that "there is no God," which is a universal negative statement. How would anyone go about proving that something does not exist?

Proof of a negative statement is difficult to pull off. For example, how would you prove the negative assertion "There is no gold in Alaska"? You would have to determine the limits of Alaska, its borders and depth and height, then dig up every cubic inch of Alaska. If there was one cubic inch you did not dig, there still might be gold there. On the other hand, how would you prove the positive assertion, "There is gold in Alaska"? Easy—you need find only one piece.

Similarly, what would you have to know in order to know for sure that there is no God? You would have to know everything. If there was one thing you did not know, that one thing might be God. We are so far from knowing everything that there is to be known, that the dogmatic assertion "There is no God" is not only not provable, it is also arrogant.

Jerry Root once asked the famous atheist Madalyn Murray O'Hair, "How much of that which there is to be known do you claim to know, 10%?" She laughed and said, "Okay, 10%." He asked, "Is it possible that God might exist and be part of that 90% of reality that you admittedly do not know?" She paused and was silent for about a minute. Then she said, "A qualified no" and quickly moved on to another question.

Often, atheists' arguments depend on rejecting in an authoritative manner any belief in God, name calling, or condescending words and attitudes to cover a deficiency of argument. They pretend to be much more certain than their arguments warrant.

Of course, the atheist can come back and maintain that there is a contradiction at the core of Christianity. This approach has been tried and found wanting.[5] Or the atheist can try to show that belief in God is improbable, but then he or she has to qualify the absolute certainty of the arguments given. Perhaps such a person would then be open to arguments from the other side, not only answering the objections made but establishing a counter case to the position being developed.

Postmodernists have rightly attacked the audacity of modernism because there is indeed much about life and reality that is not directly accessible by means of reason. However, postmodernism throws out the baby with the bath water. It is possible to retain a role for reason without being a rationalist. To reject rationalism is not necessarily to reject rationality.

DEALING WITH DOUBT

If Christianity cannot face the toughest questions people are asking today, it will be the first time in its history. The most brilliant minds through the ages have been Christian believers. Thinkers such as Augustine, Aquinas, Calvin, Edwards, Lewis and many others have time and again given able answers to recurring objections to faith.

We must acknowledge, however, that knowing all the answers to all the questions does not make us immune from doubt. This is because most of the doubts we battle are not intellectual but of emotional or spiritual origin. C. S. Lewis writes:

> Supposing a man's reason once decides that the weight of evidence is for it. I can tell that man what is going to happen to him in the next few weeks. . . . There will come a moment when he wants a woman, or wants to tell a lie, or feels very pleased with himself, or sees a chance of making a little money in some way that is not perfectly fair, some moment at which it would be convenient if Christianity were not true. And his emotions will carry out a blitz. I am not talking of any moments at which any real reasons against Christianity turn up. Those have to be faced, and that is a different matter. I am talking about moments where a mere mood rises up against it. . . Now faith in the sense in which I am using it is the art of holding onto the things your reason has once accepted, in spite of your changing moods. For moods change whatever view your reason takes.[6]

Often a person's emotional issues must be addressed before the person can sustain passionate commitment to Christ. A college student was sent to me by his Young Life leader because the student had recurring doubts about his faith. After a couple of meetings, we mutually agreed that I had answered the intellectual questions he had brought to me. However, I saw clearly that those answers would not end the student's doubt. He had been deeply hurt by his parents and by various people in his life to the extent that he had a great fear of trusting or committing himself to anyone, including God.

As we saw in chapter four, we also experience doubts, not about the existence of God but about his goodness. We encounter situations that we find to be incomprehensible. We ask, "Why are these things happening to me?" or "If God is good, would he not protect me from the kind of evil and pain I am experiencing?" Like Job, we can only trust in God who knows why. There are times it is wise to trust God even though it seems unreasonable to do so.

WILL I FLOAT OR SINK?

When my sons were ages five and seven, I taught them to swim. I got them to float on their backs with my hands supporting them, and then I gradually tried to remove my hands. Immediately they would tense up, pull up into a ball and sink. They had trouble trusting my assurance that they could—and would—really float. Such fear is similar to our distrust of God. C. S. Lewis says:

> In getting a dog out of a trap, in extracting a thorn from a child's finger, in teaching a boy to swim or rescuing one who cannot, in getting a frightened beginner over a nasty place on the mountain, the one fatal obstacle may be their distrust. . . . We ask them to believe that what is painful will relieve their pain, and that which looks dangerous is their only safety. We ask them to accept apparent impossibilities: that moving the paw further back into the trap is the way to get it out—that hurting the finger very much more will stop the finger from hurting, that water which is obviously permeable will resist and support the body . . . that to go higher and onto an exposed ledge is the way not to fall.[7]

In other words, we have to trust someone else in order to make it through the difficulty, and we have to know why we trust the person.

With my sons, getting out a splinter or touching a loose tooth took all the capital of trust I had accumulated from earlier times. Once our oldest son, Trey, had his finger crushed by a rock. He had to have several stitches, and I had to talk him through every step of the process: the shot to numb his finger (the worst part), the stitches, and his many questions about what was happening. He got through it, and his finger healed in about a month. At the time, my son could only trust that we were trying to help him and not hurt him. Similarly, we can only know from his earlier faithfulness why we trust in God who knows why.

RATIONAL BUT NOT A RATIONALIST

Damon says, "So Lewis was saying you can be a rational person without being a rationalist."

John nods. "Reason is important, but there's more to life than we can account for by reason alone. Reason helps eliminate some of the obstacles to faith, although it can't deal with all of them."

"It begins to sound like some sort of great cosmic balancing act," says Julia, gesturing largely. "You must have faith, but there is also a place for reason. If you eliminate one or the other . . ."

Mike completes Julia's sentence for her. "You fall off the tightrope."

"So is there a safety net?" Damon asks quickly.

John reminds the group, "Remember what Lewis said about trust. Based on what we have already experienced of God, we can trust him in the confusing and frightening experiences. So I would say, yes, even if we don't ever manage to fully grasp the relationship between faith and reason, we can trust God to catch us."

Brenda, who has been uncharacteristically quiet, comments "Wow, this is getting almost poetic."

Lenae sits up straighter. "Hey, I just thought of something. This is weird.

Personally, I'd say we can't know stuff about God absolutely for sure. But I still believe in him. And Simon here thinks you can know absolutely that God doesn't exist. So he's the atheist, but he's surer than I am!" She sits back as if the effort of this thought has been a little too much for her.

A short silence follows before Simon comments, "I have to be sure. You don't have to be sure about something that's only imaginary."

"Which brings up the point that imagination was very important to C. S. Lewis," says John.

"And this time I don't even think I'll have to use my dry-erase board."

IMAGINATION

Isn't Faith Merely Imaginary?

John settles more comfortably in his chair and says, "Reason and imagination were important to Lewis because they had once been separated in his own life but were later brought together. Even in his more philosophical works, Lewis often brought in imaginative metaphors and verbal pictures to bring home his meaning."

"And even more so in his stories for children," says Brenda. "Of course that's true of all good children's literature. The meaning comes through the imagination."

Lenae protests, "Oh, why can't you just read the stories as good stories? Why does everything have to mean something?"

"Interesting point. Can imagination, which seems false or invented, point to truth?" John asks the group in general.

After a pause Damon answers, "For a long time after my parents died, I think I turned to my imagination to try to make sense of it. I'd daydream about a world where they were still alive and I was with them."

"Like you could bring them back?" Julia asks gently.

"That's what's strange. It wasn't that they had come back; it was that we had all gone—someplace else. Someplace infinitely better than here. A world where people couldn't die."

Simon is quick to say, *"Heaven has always played a big part in religious people's imagination. I mean—in your mind you painted that picture because . . . well, if you want to believe it's real, and that helps you, that's OK, but . . ."* For the first time Simon seems flustered.

John says, *"Some people would say that imagination is an escape from reality, that when we imagine things, we're fooling ourselves. Certainly we can read fictional stories or make up imaginary worlds simply to escape the unpleasantness or boredom of life. On the other hand, C. S. Lewis believed that stories can be an escape to reality."*

Mike, about to take a sip of coffee, lowers his coffee mug and says, *"Wait a minute. If we're escaping to reality, where have we been? In unreality?"*

"Some of us, yes," John says with a laugh. *"Let's take a look at the role of imagination in Lewis's life. Maybe he can help us see the possibilities of imagination as a means to truth."*

REALITY: GRIM AND MEANINGLESS?

A vital step toward C. S. Lewis's conversion to Christ was what he later called the "baptism of his imagination." While on a train journey as a young man, Lewis was reading George MacDonald's fantasy *Phantastes*. As he read, he felt a strange new quality bearing upon his imagination. He called this new quality "a bright shadow" and said that it leaped off the page. Whatever this quality was, it drew the young man like a magnet. Later he identified this new quality as "holiness." That night, he says, his imagination was "baptized," although, he said, "the rest of me, not unnaturally, took longer."[1]

Imagination had always been of great value to Lewis, whether in the study of ancient mythology or in modern novels. But as he grew stronger in his atheism, he began to feel the tension of a contradiction between his reason and his imagination. That which he passionately loved in the realm of imagination—aspirations to meaning, dignity, immortality, beauty and contact with the supernatural—were what drew him into the writings of poets, philosophers and saints. Yet his rationalistic atheism forced him to deny the reality and significance of those very ideas. He describes the tension in *Surprised by Joy:*

> Such then was the state of my imaginative life; over against it stood the life of my intellect. The two hemispheres of my mind were in the sharpest contrast. On the one side a many-islanded sea of poetry and myth; on the other a glib and shallow "rationalism." Nearly all that I loved I believed to be imaginary; nearly all that I believed to be real I thought grim and meaningless.[2]

POINTING TO SOMETHING REAL

Lewis arrived at the logical conclusion of his atheism: he lived in a grim and meaningless universe. Atheist Bertrand Russell made a similar observation that atheists must build their lives on the basis of "unyielding despair."

Lewis was confronted with a dilemma. Could his reason and his imagination be reconciled? Were the things he loved—all the aspirations to meaning and goodness—only empty shells of ideas with no reality? Or did his aspirations point him to something real?

Even the books he so loved began to push him to acknowledge something beyond his atheism. He wrote:

> All the books were beginning to turn against me. Indeed, I must have been blind as a bat not to have seen, long before, the ludicrous contradiction between my theory of life and my actual ex-

periences as a reader. George MacDonald had done more to me than any other writer; of course it was a pity he had that bee in his bonnet about Christianity. He was good in spite of it. Chesterton had more sense than all the other moderns put together; bating, of course, his Christianity. Johnson was one of the few authors whom I felt I could trust utterly; curiously enough, he had the same kink. Spenser and Milton by strange coincidence had it too. Even among ancient authors the same paradox was to be found. The most religious (Plato, Aeschylus, Virgil) were clearly those on whom I could really feed. On the other hand, those writers who did not suffer from religion and with whom in theory my sympathy ought to have been complete—Shaw and Wells and Mill and Gibbon and Voltaire—all seemed a little thin; what as boys we called "tinny." It wasn't that I didn't like them. They were all (especially Gibbon) entertaining; but hardly more. There seemed to be no depth in them. They were too simple. The roughness and density of life did not appear in their books. . . . The upshot of it all could nearly be expressed in a perversion of Roland's great line in the *Chanson*—"*Christians are wrong, but all the rest are bores.*"[3]

What a radically different conclusion from that reached by many critics of Christianity who are quick to write off the Christian faith as dull and unimaginative! In the writers Lewis mentioned we find rich insight into life, a winsome moral sensibility, a great sense of humor, eloquent language, noble advice and a compelling vision of life. They delve into all the areas of reason and experience that make up the "roughness and density" of life. Consider others whom Lewis did not mention: Dostoyevsky, Tolstoy, Kierkegaard. They were fascinated by Christ and wrestled with the good and evil that infects nations as well as the human heart. Were they whistling in the dark, making up their own fantasy world? Or were they onto something real?

Lewis still needed to confront certain rational objections to the Christian faith—and, most important, finally submit his will to what he had discovered. Imagination opened his mind to the beauty of the holiness around him and ultimately to the beauty of the holiness of God.

IS IMAGINATION UNREALISTIC?

But isn't imaginative fiction a juvenile and even escapist sort of writing? Lewis's Chronicles of Narnia and Tolkien's *The Hobbit* or *The Lord of the Rings* have been labeled childish or escapist or both. For instance, when Tolkien first published *The Fellowship of the Ring* in December 1953, he wrote in a letter "I am dreading the publication for it will be impossible not to mind what is said. I have exposed my heart to be shot at."[4] As it turned out, the reviews ranged from high praise to outright contempt. American writer and critic Edmund Wilson called the book "juvenile trash." Poet and novelist Edwin Muir described it as "childish." Others faulted the work for being "unrealistic" and "escapist."

In response to the charge that fairy stories like *The Lord of the Rings* or The Chronicles of Narnia were childish, C. S. Lewis distinguished between fairy tales and children's stories. He pointed out that many children do not like fairy tales, while many adults do, and that a good story is a good story no matter what the reader's age. "Children's" stories retain their appeal throughout the generations. Lewis says:

Fashions in literary taste come and go among adults, and every period has its own shibboleths. These, when good, do not corrupt it, for children read only to enjoy. Of course, their limited vocabulary and general ignorance make some books unintelligible to them. But apart from that juvenile taste is simply human taste.[5]

Lewis felt that to grow into adulthood without developing your imagination was to be impoverished. One five-year-old boy who visited Lewis's home outside Oxford during the bombing of London in World War II had never been exposed to fairy tales. Lewis lamented that "his poor imagination has been left without any natural food at all."[6] He felt that it was important for adults to keep a childlike outlook on the world: "Only those adults who have retained with whatever additions and enrichments, their first childish responses to poetry unimpaired can be said to have grown up at all."[7] In *Experiment in Criticism* Lewis wrote, "But who in his right mind would not keep if he could that tireless curiosity, that intensity of imagination, that faculty of suspending belief, that unspoiled appetite, that readiness to wonder, to pity, to admire?"[8]

Lewis's friend Ruth Pitter said that Lewis had a child's sense of glory and nightmare. Lewis said about himself, "Parts of me are still twelve, and I think parts were already fifty when I was twelve." In any case, the capacity to avoid being hardened by cynicism and suspicion was regarded by Lewis as essential to human well-being.

Let me add a personal observation that I have met people of every age—from five to eighty-five—who have enjoyed The Chronicles of Narnia and *The Lord of the Rings*. People of any age, as long as they retain something of their childlikeness, can appreciate the stories. When I read The Chronicles of Narnia to my own sons, I found that I was more excited by rereading the stories myself than the boys were to hear them. As an adult I could better understand the many layers of meaning within the stories.

To the charge that fantasy is escapism, Tolkien responded very clearly: Yes, you might say that fantasy is escapist, but that is its glory. When a soldier is captured by the enemy, do we not consider it his duty to escape? Similarly, many self-styled culture shapers would put us all into their prison of conformity. If we value our freedom and desire liberty, then it is our duty to escape and take as many with us as we can. In "On Fairy Stories" Tolkien wrote:

> Why should a man be scorned if when finding himself in prison, he tries to get out and go home? Or, if when he cannot do so, he thinks and talks about other topics than jailers and prison walls? The world outside has not become less real because the prisoner cannot see it. In using escape in this way the critics have chosen the wrong word, and what is more, they are confusing . . . the escape of the prisoner with the flight of the deserter.[9]

ESCAPE TO REALITY

To escape from a false view of reality to a truer view of reality is not an escape from reality but an escape to reality. James Schall, in an essay titled "On the Reality of Fantasy," observes that when reading fantasy he often finds himself "pondering the state of his own soul."[10] In a similar way, novelist Stephen Lawhead maintains that the

> best of fantasy offers not an escape from reality but an escape to a heightened reality. . . . In the very best fantasy literature like *The Lord of the Rings*, we escape into an ideal world where ideal heroes and heroines (who are really only parts of our true selves) behave ideally. The work describes human life as it might be lived, perhaps ought to be lived, against a backdrop, not of all happiness and light, but of crushing difficulty and overwhelming distress.[11]

The same comments could be applied to The Chronicles of Narnia. Perhaps the enormous positive response to *The Lord of the Rings* book and films and to The Chronicles of Narnia is because these stories touch something deep in our humanity as created in the image of God. We see ordinary characters doing extraordinary acts of courage, and we begin to believe we can do the same. A writer does not have to be moralistic in order to create moral stories. Good stories show how life is to be lived—fighting against the domination of evil forces and sacrificing comfort, a finger or even life if necessary.

ORTHODOXY: THE ULTIMATE REBELLION

"Moral imagination" (a term used by writers such as Edmund Burke and Russell Kirk) has crept back into our vocabulary. It refers to the concept that we learn more when we catch a vision of the beauty of the moral life through our imagination than when we learn through lists of rules. We may read the Ten Commandments, but our hearts may not be captured by the words. Only when we see the beauty of life lived as it ought to be lived are we captivated by it. A good biography may reveal the beauty of the moral life, but other times we see it best through the bold and adventurous lives of fictional characters, whether in Narnia or in Middle Earth.

The moral life—adventurous? It hardly fits the stereotype of the prim and proper religious do-gooder. But who leads the most adventurous life? The rebel who makes a joke of traditional morality and scorns outmoded values? Such a rebellion turns out to be only conformity to the ancient drive for autonomy and personal freedom.

So if we are going to rebel, two ways are open to us. Shall we rebel in the dull conventional way? Or are we ready for a unique rebellion? The ultimate rebellion against the dominant cultural worldview is Christian orthodoxy: the Christian faith as passed down to us through the ages and expressed in the Scriptures and in the living Word of God, Jesus Christ. This may be the last genuine rebellion left to us—to dare to oppose the prevailing opinions of the day and stand for that which is timeless and eternal.

Faith in Christ is life-affirming; it is creation-enjoying. Faith in Christ is not opposed to life but to sin; it is not opposed to the creation but to the Fall. Sadly, some Christians are so afraid of sin that they fail to affirm that God has given us the whole creation to enjoy. Recovery of moral imagination involves reading stories that show how life is to be lived, and writing new ones to demonstrate that the moral life is winsome, full of life and enjoyment, and ultimately the most adventurous way to live.

SUBCREATORS UNDER GOD

God is the great Creator, but he delegates creativity to us as well. Tolkien and Lewis talked about our role as "subcreators." Only God creates something out of literally nothing, but we can use our creativity to create something out of something. We are called to exercise dominion over the whole earth as image bearers of God. To do this we must put our God-given creativity to work.

For example, an artist takes clay or marble and makes it into a statue. When I was about fifteen years old, I saw Michelangelo's statue of Moses. I had never heard of it, but I stood there overwhelmed. To me, Moses looked as though he was ready to stand up and walk away to lead the people of God. I could never again read the book of Exodus without seeing that noble and vigorous figure in my mind.

Like a sculptor, a writer creates images that stir the reader's mind years afterward. Lewis felt that to neglect imaginative reading was to limit him to the bounds of a tiny universe. The best way to read,

Lewis said, is to "Look. Listen. Receive. Get yourself out of the way."[12] Contrary to the method of some postmodern literary critics, Lewis called us to suspend judgment until after we read, so we feel and experience the world through the author's eyes. When we read what others have invented, we can travel to places we have never been, experience things we have never guessed at, struggle with dilemmas we have not yet faced, and learn how people of other cultures deal with life.

MORAL STORIES

"So it's OK if I got my sense of right and wrong by listening to 'The Lone Ranger' on the radio," Mike wonders aloud.

John answers, "I think Lewis would approve of that! As long as the masked man's values lined up with the teachings of Christ. Ultimately, of course, Lewis would want you to go to Christ himself. But I'll bet those stories you heard on the radio introduced you to the idea that there was a difference between right and wrong, and right was the better choice."

Lenae protests, "But some of us weren't raised with those absolute ideas of good and bad, right and wrong, heroes and villains. The world is more complicated now. Nobody can say for sure what's right and wrong."

"You make right and wrong for yourself," Julia tells her.

Simon flings a challenge at John. "OK, what would Mr. Lewis say about that? And don't tell me he dodged the question."

Brenda says, "I don't think Lewis ever dodged a question. But look here. This fits with what I've always believed about the Bible. The Bible is a collection of really good, well-told, imaginative stories. We take from them whatever meaning we want, and that's all we need. We don't have to believe that they really happened."

"What parts would you like to think didn't happen, Brenda?" Damon asks.

Brenda hesitates, as though this is a new thought. "Well, like people walking on water or raising dead people or waving their arms and making the Dead Sea part."

John hears Mike mutter "Red Sea" and chooses to let it go. "Do you mean the miracles in the Bible? You wonder how they can be true?"

"Yes. Yes. I guess that is what I mean. I can be a good person without believing that the law of gravity or other natural laws just quit working every now and then."

"Just listen. He's going to tell us that C. S. Lewis had the same problem," Lenae suggests.

John assumes a look of mock astonishment. "How did you guess?"

MIRACLES

But Do You Believe in the
Miracles of the Bible?

W hat do you think of when I say the word miracle?" John asks the group.

Immediately Lenae responds, "Something you don't expect to happen. Like, it'd be a miracle if I won the lottery."

Julia says, "I think it's more than that. You could win the lottery if you got the right number. The odds are against you, but it's still possible. A miracle is something more. It's something that comes to us from beyond this world."

"You don't mean—space ships and aliens?" Lenae asks with a nervous laugh.

"No, no, I mean an event that can't happen, but it does. Let's say a person has a terminal illness, and it looks hopeless. And suddenly, for no apparent reason, the person gets well. The doctors are mystified. It can't be explained scientifically."

"*You mean it can't be explained scientifically yet,*" Simon corrects her. "*Eventually science will arrive at one grand theory of the universe that will explain all physical phenomena. Until then, ignorant people will call it a miracle.*"

"*Hmm, seems there's a lot of smart ignorant people around,*" Mike comments. Quickly Simon amends his statement. "*I don't mean ignorant as in stupid, I mean . . .*"

John suggests, "*You mean they just don't know better,*" and Simon nods vigorously.

Damon, who has been quiet so far, says, "*As a kid, I'm sure I prayed to God that my parents would come back. Of course now I know it was just a childish wish, that it was impossible. Do you think, when Lewis's mother died, that he prayed for a miracle, that she would come back?*"

Brenda says, "*I think he must have. Any child would. That's why I think in many ways children are wiser than we are. They have such a simple faith. If only we didn't have to grow up and face reality.*"

"*I'm sure Lewis thought he had finally faced reality when he became an atheist,*" John suggests. "*For a number of years he fervently believed that miracles cannot possibly happen. If that were true, of course, it would be a big problem for Christianity, since miracles are one of the classic ways that Christians have provided evidence for their faith.*"

"*So what changed Lewis's mind?*" Brenda asks. "*He saw somebody walk on water?*"

"*Not exactly. Let's find out what brought Lewis around to the belief that miracles can happen—and do.*"

HERETIC IN REVERSE

C. S. Lewis gained attention beyond his academic circles through his unflinching affirmation of the supernatural—God, demons, miracles and all. How could a sophisticated Oxford professor believe in such fables in the twentieth century? When Lewis appeared on the front of *Time* magazine in 1947, the caption read, "Oxford's C. S. Lewis: His Heresy: Christianity." Historically, a heretic has been one who challenges traditional religious beliefs. Lewis was a heretic in reverse. He dared to reject the prevailing theology that lowered the bar of Christian belief, minimizing what a person needed to believe in order to embrace Christianity.

German theologian Friedrich Schleiermacher (1768-1834) had reinterpreted the Christian faith to make it palatable for its "cultured despisers." Rather than answer their objections, he gave ground and tried to eliminate inconvenient obstacles to belief such as miracles and the supernatural. The theology that descended from Schleiermacher presented a Christianity largely empty of miracles. It might be possible to accept a huge dramatic miracle such as the resurrection, but one could deny the virgin birth and the miracles Jesus performed, such as turning water into wine, walking on water and feeding the five thousand.

Lewis took on the task of considering whether it was intellectually honest and realistic to automatically reject miracles. He did not get into the details of arguing about whether particular miracles happened. Instead, he critiqued naturalism, which claims that miracles were impossible or at least so improbable that they can never be accepted.

Naturalism self-destructs. Lewis begins his book *Miracles* with a section on naturalism—nature is all there is. We can represent naturalism and supernaturalism in these terms: *naturalism* presents nature as a closed box with everything explained by natural cause and effect; *supernaturalism* sees nature as an open system, operating by natural law most of the time but open to intervention by God.

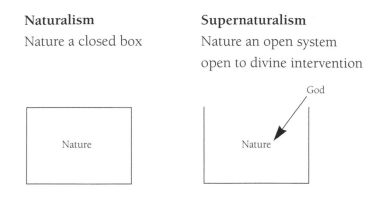

Figure 8.1.

Lewis's strategy was to demonstrate that naturalism would eventually self-destruct. If naturalism is true, then we cannot be certain of the arguments that attempt to establish it.

The argument goes like this: in order for naturalism to be true, it must account for everything under the naturalistic premise. Yet the one thing naturalism cannot account for is the reasoning process, which is necessary to establish naturalism. If a theory provides an explanation for everything in the universe but undermines the very thinking used to establish it, then it would disprove the theory or at least make it highly suspect. If naturalism undermines reason itself, Lewis says: "It would have destroyed its own credentials. It would be an argument which proved that no argument was sound—a proof that there are no such things as proofs—which is nonsense."[1]

Lewis says that naturalism "offers what professes to be a full account of our mental behavior; but this account, on inspection leaves no room for the acts of knowing or insight on which the whole value of our thinking, as a means of truth, depend."[2]

If only blind, unconscious material forces are working by chance within the closed box of nature, then how do we explain the conscious thinking beings who arise out of that chance process? According to naturalism, we are chance products of that box and cannot get outside it. Material forces, working by chance, might produce an ability to think in a way that was sound, but more likely they would give us defective, distorted reasoning abilities.

Cosmic dice. In *Reason to Believe* Richard Purtill, professor emeritus of philosophy at Western Washington University, restates Lewis's argument (taking critiques of it into account):

> If I pose a mathematical problem and throw some dice, the dice might happen to fall into a pattern which gives the answer to my problem. But there is no reason to suppose that they will. Now in the Chance view, all our thoughts are the results of processes as random as a throw of dice. . . . [A]ll our thoughts result from processes that have as little relation to our minds as the growth of a tree."[3]

If you throw the dice to get the solution to your math problem, how likely is it that the first or second throw would give you the right answer? The complexity of the universe is far greater than 2 + 2 = 4. It will always be more likely that you will come up with an erroneous result than the true one.

Lewis presents us with much more than a math problem: the question of validity of human reasoning. Even if somehow our reasoning powers were valid, we would never know or have an adequate basis to know it. Thus on a naturalistic foundation, all our confidence in the reason used to establish naturalism is undermined. Our only slim hope is that one in a billion rolls of the dice has produced the correct result.

SOCRATIC CLUB DEBATE

In 1948, as part of the regular Socratic Club meeting at Oxford, Elizabeth Anscombe, an analytic philosopher, brought forward some critiques of Lewis's argument in chapter three of *Miracles*. Without going into all the details, the general thrust of the debate went as follows. In the original version of *Miracles*, which Anscombe was critiquing, Lewis had slightly overstated his case. He had argued that when we find that a belief results from chance, we discount it. Anscombe pointed out, in essence, that a belief arising from nonrational sources just might happen to give a right answer. She asked Lewis: "What is the connection between grounds and the actual occurrence of the belief?"

Lewis made some qualifications to his position and later felt that the points raised by Anscombe warranted some revisions to this early section of *Miracles*. What is surprising about this incident is the "much ado" made about it. Some say that Lewis lost the debate, some say he won it, and others are in between. For instance, philosopher Basil Mitchell, who was present, said in an interview, "I don't have the sense that anything decisive happened at that moment."[1] Much has been made of Lewis's psychological state after the debate. Some say he was crushed by it; others, including Anscombe herself, who had dinner with him not long afterward, said that Lewis was his normal jovial self. Some claim that he gave up writing apologetics after the debate; others say that is absurd. Interestingly, one of the strongest critics of Lewis, John Beversluis, critiques A. N. Wilson's biography and his own earlier account by saying: "It is simply untrue that the post-Anscombe Lewis abandoned Christian apologetics." After giving several examples of such writings, he says: "It is rhetorically effective to announce that the post-Anscombe Lewis wrote no further books on Christian apologetics, but it is pure fiction."[5] For instance,

Lewis later responded to Norman Pittinger's critique of his arguments on miracles in *The Christian Century*. Jerry Root, coauthor of *The Quotable Lewis*, maintains that about half of Lewis's apologetic essays, including his important essay on "Christian Apologetics," were written after the debate.

Probably it is best is to say that Lewis, although once a philosophy tutor, was more trained in the classic philosophical tradition than in the new analytic philosophy. He knew that in order to further debate with philosophers such as Anscombe, he would have to do much further study, for which he had no particular inclination. So he decided to write more in other areas and not do much further work in the philosophical arena.

The central question is, was his argument in *Miracles* sound? I think the answer is yes. A few years later, John Lucas set up a debate with Elizabeth Anscombe on the same issues and defended Lewis's position to the satisfaction of many. Philosopher Basil Mitchell (later president of the Socratic Club) said about this rerun debate between Lucas and Anscombe:

> Lucas simply maintained that on the substantial issue, Lewis was right and that, for the sort of reasons Lewis had put forward, a thoroughly naturalistic philosophy was logically incoherent. An outcome of that debate was to make it perfectly clear that, at the very least, Lewis's original thesis was an entirely arguable philosophical thesis and as defensible as most philosophical theses are.[6]

A logical proof. Philosopher Victor Reppert has written an excellent book, *C. S. Lewis's Dangerous Idea: A Philosophical Defense of Lewis's Argument from Reason*. He argues that Lewis's argument from reason is dangerous to naturalism because it undermines it altogether. He restates Lewis's argument, taking into account criticisms made against it:

1. No belief is rationally inferred if it can be fully explained in terms of nonrational causes.

2. If materialism is true, then all beliefs can be explained in terms of nonrational causes.

3. Therefore, if materialism is true, then no belief is rationally inferred.

4. If any thesis entails the conclusion that no belief is rationally inferred, then it should be rejected and its denial accepted.

5. Therefore, materialism should be rejected and its denial accepted.[7]

Reppert then proceeds to philosophically defend this argument against all philosophical objections. He defended his Ph.D. dissertation on this subject before a committee who were hostile to his conclusion, but despite this he passed.

Reppert maintains that the argument from reason can bear up under the weight of the most serious philosophical attacks. It is an argument that deserves our attention, especially as we deal with those who try to explain all human aspirations in terms of survival value and biology.

MIRACLES

There are three negative ways to respond to miracles: they are (1) impossible, (2) improbable or (3) inappropriate. Lewis addresses all three of these objections.

Impossible? Many people assume that miracles are impossible. Lewis says in *Reflections on the Psalms:* "The real reason why I can accept as historical a story in which a miracle occurs is that I have never found any philosophical grounds for the universal negative proposition that miracles don't happen."[8]

Unless we are absolutely certain that there is no supernatural power (God) in the universe, we cannot dogmatically say that every claim of a miracle is false. Granted, miracles are rare. They are foreign to our everyday experience. It does not follow that miracles are impossible. We can never assume that what we have experienced is all there is to reality.

Improbable? A common philosophical argument against miracles is based on their improbability. David Hume maintained that it is always more likely that any particular claim to a miracle is false than that the miracle actually took place. In other words, in light of the "firm and unalterable" laws of nature, it is always easier to believe that those who testify to a miracle are in error than that they are telling the truth. For instance, there are billions of instances in which dead people stay dead and only occasional stories of dead people rising. The odds would be several billion to one (or two or three or so on) against such a report being true.

When I was in graduate school, I took part in the regular meetings of a group called Apologia, which consisted of a number of believing graduate students from various disciplines. I remember spending many hours on Hume's philosophical critique of miracles. The more we explored the argument, the stranger it seemed to me. I asked one philosopher who had been deeply affected by this argument, "What if five hundred people were claimed to have risen from the dead and five thousand people in each case were said to have witnessed the resurrection, would that bring a different result?" I was assured that, no, it would still be several billion versus five thousand in each case. It would not matter if I and all my friends witnessed one hundred miracles; the result would still be the same. As I thought about it, the question emerged: "Why do the instances that establish natural law have to count against a reported miracle?" Rather than weighing the evidence for a miracle, the skeptics used natural law—the usual way things work—to exclude the unusual (the miracle). Lewis says:

> Now of course we must agree with Hume that if there is absolutely "uniform experience" against miracles, if in other words they have never happened, why then they never have. Unfortunately we know the experience against them to be uniform only if we know that all the reports of them are false. And we can know all the reports to be false only if we know already that miracles have never occurred. In fact, we are arguing in a circle.[9]

No instance of a miracle is allowed by Hume because another explanation is always preferable to him, such as, in Lewis's words, "Collective hallucination, hypnotism of unconsenting spectators, widespread instantaneous conspiracy. . . . Such a procedure is, from the purely historical point of view, sheer midsummer madness unless we start by knowing that any miracle whatever is more improbable than the most improbable natural event. Do we know this?"[10]

Another of Hume's arguments against the miraculous is that people from earlier ages were uneducated and uncivilized and therefore easily duped by miracle claims. Even if people of the past knew less than we know, we cannot discount everything they reported as true. People throughout history have known that the dead do not normally rise and virgins do not normally have babies. When Joseph learned of Mary's pregnancy, he was ready to break his engagement with her. He was under no illusions that virgin births regularly happen. Only a supernatural encounter persuaded Joseph otherwise (Matthew 1:18-25).

Inappropriate? Another of Hume's arguments against miracles is that various competing religions make miracle claims to give credibility to their views. Lewis's approach to this argument is first to admit the possibility that some of the miracle claims outside Christianity are true. Perhaps God could heal someone in a pagan religion, not to establish that religion's claims but merely out of compassion. Lewis writes in *Miracles:* "I do not think that it is the duty of the Christian apologist (as many skeptics suppose) to disprove all stories of the miraculous which fall outside the Christian records. . . . I am in no way committed to the assertion that God has never worked miracles through and for Pagans or never permitted created supernatural beings to do so."[11]

Having admitted the possibility of the miraculous among non-Christians, Lewis argues for the unique "fitness" or appropriateness of miracles within Christianity: "But I claim that the Christian miracles have a much greater intrinsic probability in virtue of their organic connection with one another and with the whole structure of the religion they exhibit."[12]

In Hinduism, for example, the principle of nondistinction (all is One) rules out the validity of any distinction between natural and supernatural. In that case miracles—interventions of the supernatural into the natural—are meaningless because there is no line between natural and supernatural.

There are stories in late Buddhism about miracles performed by the Buddha. But since he taught that nature is illusory, why would he need to demonstrate power over the illusion? One early story includes Buddha's discussion with a man who was sitting by a lake meditating so that he could walk across on the water. Buddha's advice was to take the ferry.[13] After all, craving for magical power could hinder enlightenment (freedom from all desires). Lewis comments:

Sometimes the credibility of the miracles is in an inverse ratio to the credibility of the religion. Thus miracles are (in late documents, I believe) recorded of the Buddha. But what could be more absurd than that he who came to teach us that Nature is an illusion from which we must escape should occupy himself in producing effects on the Natural level—that he who comes to wake us from a nightmare should add to the nightmare? The more we respect his teaching the less we could accept his miracles.[14]

Later stories about the Buddha flying and shooting sparks, far from helping the cause of Buddhism, actually hindered it by going against Buddha's teaching.[15]

So miracles do not have the same place and significance—the same fitness—in pantheism or paganism as they have in theism. In Christianity miracles have decisive significance, converging on Christ and demonstrating that he is the one sent by God. In the Old Testament, miracles are present around agents of revelation or as a means of deliverance of God's people (as at the Red Sea), but they do not have the same focus as in the New Testament (on Christ himself). Even in the Qur'an, Jesus is reported to have done miracles, while Muhammad does none, except the revelation of the Qur'an itself. Only in later Islamic tradition do we find reports of miracles done by Muhammad.

As Lewis says, miracles in the New Testament are greater in their "intrinsic probability" because of the credibility of their historic claims (discussed in chap. 5 on myth and in reference books in the "Recommended Reading" section) and because of their "organic connection"—how they fit together and converge on Jesus Christ. The miracles of Christ are not merely powerful acts for the sake of power;

they demonstrate his identity. His healing of the man born blind (John 9) leads to the revelation that Jesus is the light of the world. The resurrection of Lazarus from the dead (John 11) leads to the proclamation that Jesus is the resurrection and the life. The miracles fit within the whole of the Christian faith.

SUMMARY

To those who would deny the miraculous, C. S. Lewis would say:

- Naturalists (those who view nature as a closed box) cannot sustain their position because their own assumptions undermine the credibility of their thinking.

- Miracles are not impossible. There is no argument to prove that miracles cannot happen.

- Miracles are not improbable, unless you wrongly oppose natural law and supernatural events. You need to weigh the historical evidence for each unusual event before you exclude or accept it.

- Miracles are not inappropriate. In comparison with other religions, there is a unique "fitness" to miracles in Christianity.

THE WILL TO BELIEVE

Brenda presses one hand to her forehead, a thinking gesture, and says, "So these theologians tried to say Christians don't need to believe in miracles, but Lewis said they do?"

Lenae asks, "Why make it harder than it has to be?"

"I think because Lewis cared about the truth. He wanted us to be brave enough to look all truth in the face, even if it's difficult," John replies.

Simon voices a complaint, "Yeah, and he also said that the thought processes of naturalists—my thought processes!—are suspect because they're just a result of random chance."

Damon says, "No, you say your thought processes are just a result of random chance. Lewis simply pointed out how you naturalists contradict yourselves."

"Well, I still don't believe in miracles," Simon declares and folds his arms.

"Your privilege," Mike says and folds his arms in imitation.

Quickly John responds, "Simon, you've made an excellent point. We've talked about some of the obstacles Lewis faced on his journey to faith. We need to remember that he could have allowed any one of them stop him. He could have persisted in his atheism. But he decided to let himself be persuaded and to go on to the next step."

"So what's our next step?" Julia asks. "As I told you before, for me this is all part of an ongoing journey."

"Well, Lewis wouldn't want us to consider each of these ideas in isolation and leave it at that. He was committed to the fact that Christianity fits the whole of life. In his view people come to believe not when one thing seems to prove that faith is credible but when everything confirms it. So I thought next week we'd start taking a look at how—according to Lewis—faith in Christ fits everything in a comprehensive sense. That is, if you're all still with me."

John looks around the circle. Lenae, Julia, Mike, Brenda, Damon and Simon all nod their heads, though some more enthusiastically than others.

PART THREE

COHERENCE

Does It All Fit Together?

9

WISH FULFILLMENT

Isn't Belief in God
Just a Crutch for Needy People?

The following week John is relieved to see all six members of the group arrive on time or even a little early. He greets each one warmly. They have become important people in his life, and he is amazed at how widely they differ: Mike, the oldest of the group, who apparently holds the most traditional ideas but so far has said little about himself; Julia, who wants to construct an individualized religion for herself; Simon, who is still combative in his atheism but keeps coming back; Lenae, the youngest, being pushed to think deeply about Christian faith for the first time; Damon, confronting his questions about God, which he has avoided since the death of his parents; and Brenda, whose reasons for studying C. S. Lewis appear more complex than her interest in children's literature.

And then there's me, John tells himself, a Christian believer who prays that Lewis's writings and our discussions will draw these people closer to Christ. And that I'll be drawn there too. Amazing how Lewis continues to speak to so many people through his writings.

"Hey, John, are we going to get started?" It's Mike's voice.

"Sorry. I was just thinking—wondering—how remarkable it is that Lewis still captivates people's minds, decades after his death."

"Like I've always said, good writing is timeless," Brenda says.

Damon suggests, "I think people are still looking for what Lewis offers. Reasonable answers to their questions, and no glossing over the hard stuff."

Julia, who looks especially eager to get into the discussion this evening, asks, "So this week we're going to see how it all fits into the great wholeness of life—right?"

"Well, we'll get started anyway. Simon, I'm going to ask you to get us going." (Simon looks startled.) "You don't believe in God, but I think you'll admit that atheists are in the minority. Why do you think most people through the ages have believed in some kind of all-powerful supernatural being?"

Simon has a ready answer. "Humanity invented God out of need. Think of living in a cave with wild animals prowling outside in the dark. Think about battling woolly mammoths and saber-toothed tigers with just a spear. Primitive people lived on the edge of survival. If they could pray to somebody that was all-powerful, maybe he or she or it would help them. And of course if your tribe was at war with another tribe, you called on your god to help you defeat your enemies, who by the way were calling on their god to defeat you."

John doesn't question Simon's anthropological theories, but looks around the group with a questioning expression. Brenda comments, "Sounds like those cavemen did a lot of wishful thinking."

"Wish fulfillment is another name for it," John says. "When he was an atheist, C. S. Lewis held to a psychological explanation of religion. He thought that 'God' was something human beings invented to cope with the uncertainties of a confusing and often dangerous world."

"So I'm in good company," says Simon with a half-grudging smile.

A PSYCHOLOGICAL EXPLANATION

The psychological explanation for God is one of the most common arguments against Christian faith (and against any theistic religion). Some explanation for humanity's belief in God is necessary because empirical evidence shows that belief in a god or some supernatural power is common to all cultures in all time periods. What could be behind such a universal phenomenon? Is something so basic to human nature a vast illusion, or does it point beyond itself to a real God?

Atheists prefer to explain God as wish fulfillment, that humanity invented God because we wished God existed. Lewis portrayed the seductiveness of this idea—and a bold rebuke of it—in one of the Narnia tales, *The Silver Chair.*

In *The Silver Chair* Prince Rilian has just been freed from the enchantment of the silver chair by invoking the name of Aslan. Jill, Scrubb, Puddleglum and Prince Rilian encounter the Queen of the Underland, the Green Witch. She tries to bring all of them under her spell, throwing green powder in a fire and strumming on something like a mandolin. She is the Queen of denial. She tells them that "there is no land called Narnia," there is no "Overworld," there is no sun, no sky, and above all no Aslan. All of their minds are dulled by the enchanting power of the Witch, and they begin to believe that they have only imagined or invented these things.

Puddleglum, in an act of desperation, thrusts his foot into the fire. The smell of burned Marsh-wiggle fills the air, causing Puddleglum's mind to clear. He then says:

Suppose we *have* only dreamed, or made up, all those things—

trees and grass and sun and moon and stars and Aslan himself. Suppose we have. Then all I can say is that, in that case, the made up things seem a good deal more important than the real ones. Suppose this black pit of a kingdom of yours is the only world. Well, it strikes me as a pretty poor one. And that's a funny thing when you come to think of it. We're babies making up a game, if you're right. But four babies playing a game can make a play-world which licks your real world hollow.[1]

Three influential atheists. Three influential atheists put forward the idea that God was a psychological invention: Ludwig Feuerbach, Karl Marx and Sigmund Freud.

Ludwig Feuerbach (1804-1872), though least well-known of the three, was a German philosopher who significantly shaped the views of Marx and Freud. In his book *The Essence of Christianity* (1841), he argues that religion tells us much about humanity but nothing about God. "God" is a projection of human consciousness, and "theology is anthropology." According to Feuerbach, every supposed attribute of God can be explained by human needs.

Karl Marx (1818-1883) was fascinated by Feuerbach's thesis and took it a step further, applying it to social reform. According to Marx the ruling classes invent religion in order to keep the masses of workers content with their unjust situations. The rulers use religion for their own economic advantage. If the workers remain content and do not rock the boat, they are promised "pie in the sky," a heavenly reward. Marx believed that religion was the opiate of the people, a narcotic that dulled their pain so they could endure more oppression without revolting. Therefore religion needed to be smashed in order for the workers to wake from their narcotic dream and revolt against their oppressors.

Sigmund Freud (1856-1939) took Feuerbach's critique further in the psychological direction. He argued that belief in God was an illusion arising out of wish fulfillment.

C. S. Lewis's response. C. S. Lewis's views during his atheistic phase were certainly influenced by Freud. In *Pilgrim's Regress,* Lewis takes the reader on a fictional journey through the intellectual landscape of his era. He repeatedly pokes holes in Freud's wish-fulfillment theory.

In the story the pilgrim John seeks a beautiful island that he has seen in a vision. He has left his home in Puritania and has begun to reject his previous belief in the "Landlord" (God), his "card of rules" (Law) and the "black hole" (Hell). Along the way he encounters Sigismund Enlightenment. (Lewis knew that Freud's birth name was Sigismund, which he later changed to Sigmund.)

Sigismund (S) speaks to John (J):

S   It may save you trouble if I tell you at once the best reason for not trying to escape: namely, that there is nowhere to escape to.

J   How do you know that there is no such place as my island?

S   Do you wish very much that there were?

J   I do.

S   Have you ever imagined anything to be true because you greatly wished for it?

John thought for a while and then he said, "Yes."

S   And your island is like an imagination—isn't it?

J   I suppose so.

S   It's just the sort of thing you would imagine merely through wanting it; the whole thing is very suspicious.[2]

SOME THINGS WE WISH FOR DO EXIST

Wishing for something does not make it true or real. On the other hand the wish itself does not prove that what we desire does not exist. If you are hungry, you wish for food. Fortunately food exists to satisfy your wish. If you are thirsty, you wish for something to drink. There are various beverages to satisfy your thirst. Sleep meets the desire to rest, and sex fulfills sexual desire.

But what about other more abstract desires? Do our deep human yearnings and aspirations point toward a real future fulfillment? Or are they inevitably doomed to frustration? Are our longings for meaning, dignity, immortality and spiritual experience only a row of dead-end streets? Or are these and other such aspirations destined for fulfillment? Does God put these yearnings into our conscience because we are made in his image? Or must we, with B. F. Skinner, outgrow such confining ideas and go "beyond freedom and dignity."[3]

Before he came to Christ, C. S. Lewis experienced sharp longings for something mystically above and beyond his ordinary life. These experiences haunted him until he came to faith in Christ, and then they took a back seat to the new reality he enjoyed. The desires were like signs by the roadside, of great interest in navigating his way to the destination but of little significance once he arrived. He wrote in *Mere Christianity:*

> The longings which arise in us when we first fall in love, or first think of some foreign country, or first take up some subject that really excites us, are longings which no marriage, no travel, no learning, can really satisfy. I am not now speaking of that which would be ordinarily called unsuccessful marriages, or holidays, or learned careers. I am speaking of the best possible ones. There was something we grasped, at that first moment of longing, which just fades away in the reality.[4]

Lewis argues that there are three ways of dealing with these facts—two wrong ways and one right way. First, "the fool's way" involves putting the blame on the things that fail to provide permanent satisfaction and imagining that lasting joy can be achieved if you find something better than you have had. You could try a different wife, another vacation destination, another house or car, looking for what will finally and fully satisfy. People like this tend to "spend their whole lives trotting from woman to woman (through the divorce courts), from continent to continent, from hobby to hobby, always thinking that the latest is the real thing at last, and always disappointed."[5]

Second is "the way of the disillusioned 'sensible man,' " that is, the cynic. Cynics do not expect much and therefore are not disappointed when they do not get it. They repress the part of themselves that would "cry for the moon."[6] Lewis suggests that cynicism might be the best approach for those who disbelieve in eternal life and any future satisfaction of our deepest desires.

Third, "the Christian way" maintains that "Creatures are not born with desires unless satisfaction for these desires exists." Just as hunger points to food and sexual desire points to sex, "if I find in myself a desire which no experience in this world can satisfy, the most probable explanation is that I was made for another world." Just because the things I desire on earth do not fully satisfy, this "does not prove the universe is a fraud." Our pleasures here on earth act as cosmic pointers to those realities that will ultimately satisfy us. The problem is that we mistake the temporary things for the eternal, when they are "only a kind of copy, or echo, or mirage." Lewis says: "I must keep alive in myself the desire for my true country which I shall not find till after death. . . . I must make it the main object of life to press on to that other country and to help others do the same."[7]

Does All of Our Reasoning Come from Nonrational Forces?

The theory that religion is only wish fulfillment rests on the assumption that we cannot count on our thought processes to be rational. The view is self-refuting, as Lewis shows in *Pilgrim's Regress,* where Reason (R) and John (J) dialogue:

R   The Spirit of the Age wishes to allow argument and not allow argument.

J   How is that?

R   You heard what they said. If anyone argues with them they say that he is rationalizing his own desires, and therefore need not be answered. But if anyone listens to them, they will argue themselves to show that their own doctrines are true.

J   I see. And what is the cure for this?

R   You must ask them whether any reasoning is valid or not. If they say no, then their own doctrines, being reached by reasoning, fall to the ground. If they say yes, then they will have to examine your arguments and refute them on their merits. For, if some reasoning is valid, for all they know, your bit of reasoning may be one of the valid bits.[8]

As a historical example of the argument from nonrationality, Karl Marx was a strict materialist. He claimed that all ideas arise out of matter, particularly the economic aspect of matter. He also claimed that the ruling classes created religion for their own economic benefit. Yet Marx unfairly exempted himself from his own argument.

Lewis prods us to ask: Is all reasoning determined by matter, or not? If all ideas arise only from materialistic economic forces, how can Marx give us an objective statement about religion, or about anything else, unaffected by his own economic interests? Marx and his followers cannot have it both ways. If their ideas are valid and somehow undetermined by matter, then perhaps other ideas—like religious and cultural ideas—are valid as well. Either Marx's own theories are negated, or he opens the door to the possibility that other theories are true.

In Freud's case, if all beliefs come out of the nonrational unconsciousness shaped by our past, is this not true of Freud's own beliefs? Either his own explanation of others' views applies to himself, or it does not. If it applies to himself, then his own views are suspect; if it does not apply to him, why not?

Bulverism. Feuerbach, Freud and Marx rejected the theistic position rather than attempting to reasonably refute it. They assumed that God does not exist and then pinned a psychological explanation on those who believe in God. They labeled religion a "projection," "wish fulfillment" and an "opiate" but neglected the most important question: Does God exist or not?

Lewis uses the analogy of a bank account to illustrate their intellectual laziness: "If you think that my claim to have a large balance is due to wishful thinking, it might be a good idea to find out whether I have such an account and determine what amount I have in it."[9] Lewis goes on to say, "In other words, you must show that a man is wrong before you start explaining why he is wrong. The modern method is to assume without discussion that he is wrong and then distract his attention from this (the only real issue) by busily explaining how he became so silly."[10]

Lewis invented the name "Bulverism" for this fallacy. He personified it in the created character Ezekiel Bulver,

> whose destiny was determined at the age of five when he heard his mother say to his father, who had been maintaining that two sides of a triangle were together greater than that of the third,

"Oh, you say that because you are a man." At that moment, E. Bulver assures us, "There flashed across my opening mind that refutation is no necessary part of an argument. Assume that your opponent is wrong, and then explain his error, and the world will be at your feet. Attempt to prove that he is wrong or (worse still) try to find out if he is wrong or right, and the rational dynamism of our age will thrust you to the wall." That is how Bulver became one of the makers of the twentieth century.[11]

If Bulverists were the makers of the twentieth century, they have a head start on the twenty-first as well. To attack people's motives rather than to refute their arguments is even more common now. Lewis said that he saw Bulverism at work in "every political argument" and warned that until "Bulverism is crushed, reason can play no effective part in human affairs."[12]

Some religious views are contrary to our wishes. If faith in God is only wish fulfillment, why does our faith include so many problematic aspects? There are Christian teachings we accept but trouble us, sometimes very deeply. At one point in *Pilgrim's Regress*, Reason asks John, "Is it really true that the giant and Sigismund, and the people in Eschropolis, and Mr. Halfways are going about filled with a longing that there should be a Landlord, and a card of rules, and a mountain land beyond the brook, with the possibility of a black hole?"[13]

Many teachings that are basic to theism and to Christian faith in particular run precisely counter to wish-fulfillment theory. Why would all people wish for a holy, righteous, just God who is angry at sin? Why would there be a universal longing for moral rules that put restrictions on our personal freedom? Who would wish for divine judgment or hell? (On our enemies perhaps, but certainly not on our friends!) Why are these troublesome religious beliefs so prevalent? Why have we not wished these ideas away?

DISBELIEF: A WISH FULFILLMENT?

Lewis argues that if you want to play the Bulverism game, you need to understand that it works both ways. Bulverism is a "truly democratic game." Lewis says:

> I see my religion dismissed on the grounds that "the comfortable parson had every reason for assuring the nineteenth century worker that poverty would be rewarded in another world." Well, no doubt he had. On the assumption that Christianity is an error, I can see easily enough that some people would have a reason for inculcating it. I can see it so easily that I can, of course, play the game the other way around, by saying that the modern man has every reason for trying to convince himself that there are no eternal sanctions behind the morality he is rejecting.[14]

Religion can be a projection of some human experience onto God. Consider how easy it is to see God in the image of our earthly father, with all of his faults. Religion can also be used as a dulling drug. We can find examples of Christian missionaries who used converts for their own economic advantage. Religion can also be wish fulfillment. Listen to those who say "my God is a God of _____" (usually love); in other words, "God" is as I wish him to be.

However, simply because we admit that religious beliefs can be abused, that does not prove that they have no right use. An argument against abuse is not an argument against use.

As Lewis indicated, the tables can be turned on the atheist. We can just as readily say:

- Atheism is a projection, a desire to kill God and be free without any accountability to a higher power.

- Atheism is an opiate of the conscience. To escape moral guilt for their sin, people can project, rationalize, justify or anesthetize it. While some people use drugs or sex to dull the pain of guilt, they could just as easily use atheism.

- Atheism is wish fulfillment. To use Freud's terms, atheism could be a giant Oedipus complex, wishing the death of the heavenly Father. In simpler terms the atheists may be wishing away morality or responsibility or the idea of letting anyone else control their lives.

For twenty years Paul Vitz was an atheist, Freudian professor of psychology at New York University before he became a Christian believer. He maintains that the above charges against atheism are accurate. But why would atheists deny what they know to be true? Why do atheists repress the truth about God?

When we repress something, at a deeper level we know it is really true. When the repressed knowledge attempts to surface in our consciousness, we fight to keep it down. In the same way Paul argues (Romans 1:18-32) that at some level everyone knows that there is a God, but when the knowledge comes to the forefront, it generates anger and hostility. We do not easily admit that we have done wrong and need a Savior.

Systematic dishonesty. If people know there is a God and at the same time deny that God exists, the internal conflict leads to a systematic dishonesty. A one point Karl Marx was informed that the facts he used in chapter eight of *Das Kapital* were in error. Yet if he deleted that section, he would delete an important part of his argument. He decided to leave that section intact even though he knew it was false.

In his book *Intellectuals* Paul Johnson says of Marx: "He can never be trusted. The whole of chapter eight of *Das Kapital* is a deliberate and systematic falsification to prove a thesis which an objective examination of the facts showed was untenable."[15] Johnson goes on to explore aspects of Marx's personality that might have led to such dishonesty. Perhaps at the root there was a bitterness and hatred which extended not only to people but also to God. Michael Bakunin's final judgment after personally observing Marx was that "Marx does not believe in God but he believes much in himself and makes everyone serve himself. His heart is not full of love, but of bitterness and he has very little sympathy for the human race."[16]

Techow, one person who knew Marx and was initially very impressed by him, had this to say:

> He was a man of outstanding personality with a rare intellectual superiority and if his heart had matched his intellect and he had possessed as much love as hate, I would have gone through the fire for him. But he is lacking in nobility of soul. I am convinced that a most dangerous ambition has eaten away all the good in him. . . . [T]he acquisition of personal power is the aim of all his endeavors.[17]

Could it be that Marx was actively projecting his hate onto the universe, using his atheism as an opiate of the conscience and wishing the death of the heavenly Father?

In recent years several books have exposed the dishonesty of some prominent modern culture shapers: *Intellectuals* by Paul Johnson; Derek Freeman's *Margaret Mead and Samoa: The Making and Unmaking of an Anthropological Myth;* Paul Vitz's *Sigmund Freud's Christian Unconscious;* David Lehman's *Signs of the Times: Deconstructionism and the Fall of Paul deMan.* We can only wonder whether the desire to maintain their atheism led these thinkers to a denial of truth in their intellectual work.

Fundamentally self-refuting. Lewis sums up his argument against Freud and Marx:

> The Freudians have discovered that we exist as bundles of complexes. The Marxians have discovered that we exist as members of some economic class. . . . Thoughts are ideologically tainted at the source. Now this is obviously great fun; but it has not always been noticed that there is a bill to pay for it. There are two questions that people who say this kind of thing ought to be asked. The first is, are all thoughts tainted at the source or only some? The second is, does the taint invalidate the tainted thought in the sense of making it untrue—or not? . . . If they say that all thoughts are thus tainted, then of course. . . . The Freudian and the Marxian are in the same boat with all the rest of us and cannot criticize us from the outside. They have sawn off the branch they are sitting on. If on the other hand, they say that the taint need not invalidate their thinking, then neither need it invalidate ours. In which case they have saved their own branch, but also saved ours along with it.[18]

Lewis concluded that Marx, Freud and others who try to explain away God "are trying to *prove* that all *proofs* are invalid. If you fail, you fail. If you succeed, then you fail even more—for the proof that all proofs are invalid must be invalid itself."[19]

To sum up Lewis's response to the wish-fulfillment theory, he might say something like this:

- Merely wishing something does not prove that the object of your wish is unreal or untrue.

- You are guilty of a logical fallacy if you assume that God does not exist and then try to explain God psychologically. That is "Bulverism," the attempt to reject rather than refute.

- Many religious beliefs are the opposite of what we desire.

- An equal or better case can be made that disbelief in God is wish fulfillment.

- Above all, the theories of Marx and Freud are ultimately self-refuting.

IF LEWIS LIVED TODAY

With some belligerence Simon demands of John, "Are you saying that everybody who chooses not to believe in God is either a communist or a Freudian?"

"Of course not! The point is simply that Marx and Freud, and Feuerbach before them, didn't play fair when they wrote off God as wishful thinking by the human race. Just because we wish for something, that doesn't make it untrue."

Julia makes a sound of impatience. "No offense, but if you ask me, I think we're spending too much time on atheism. We've already agreed that atheists are in the minority. The vast majority of the human race believes in the spirit world. I want everybody's opinion. C. S. Lewis lived out his spiritual quest back in—what was it?—the 1940s and 1950s. If he was living today and set out on his spiritual quest, what path do you think he would follow?"

John blinks in surprise. The question is unexpected. The more he thinks about it, the more it intrigues him. He waits for other group members to respond, but they remain quiet and thoughtful.

Julia answers her own question. "I think Lewis would be a postmodern renaissance man!"

"A what?" asks Lenae.

"I mean he would explore truth wherever it was to be found, not limiting himself to the holy Bible or the Church of England or whatever tradition he was raised in. Think how widely he read, how he loved to see and hear others' perspectives."

Damon ventures to say, "I don't know, he seemed pretty well committed to . . ."

"John, you've already said Lewis rejected modernism," Julia points out. "So postmodernism is the next logical step for him."

John says slowly, "He did reject modernism in the sense that reason is everything, but . . . you know, Julia, I need to think about this more, but in a way I agree with you."

"I don't!" Brenda says sharply. "It seems to me Lewis would laugh at a lot of postmodern ideas."

"I agree with you too," John says.

Mike protests, "John, you can't agree with everybody."

"I agree," says John a little sheepishly.

Mike isn't through. "I don't know who I agree with, because I don't even know what we're talking about. I've heard this word postmodern for years and I still don't know what it means. What is postmodernism?"

POSTMODERNISM

Is What Was True for C. S. Lewis
Necessarily True for Me?

John takes a deep breath and says, "We'll answer the question of what postmodernism is at greater length, but there's a succinct definition by the French philosopher Jean-François Lyotard, who lived from 1924 to 1998. He defined postmodernism as 'incredulity towards metanarratives.' "

Brenda says, "Great! Now all we have to do is figure out what metanarratives are."

"Thanks, we'll define that term next. A metanarrative is any narrative, story or account of the world that claims to be absolute or all encompassing."

Lenae asks tentatively, "You mean like—'the world is round'?"

"More like the story of the world you read in your high school history text," John says. "Well, probably not your high school history text, but definitely mine. Or Mike's."

Damon asks plaintively, "Aren't we getting away from C. S. Lewis?"

"Well, Lewis lived before the full flowering of postmodern thought, but *some of its roots were already present in his day. First let's look at what postmodernism is, and then we'll consider what Lewis's response to it might be. He would agree with some aspects of this philosophy and disagree with others."*

CAN WE KNOW ANYTHING?

In the traditional approach to history, writers attempt to construct a reasonable and coherent story to explain the sweep of historical events. Postmodernists are skeptical of this approach to history, not only because of the limits of human understanding but because they regard the authors of such metanarratives as oppressors who silenced the voices of the minority and the defeated. In other words the conquerors, not the conquered, control what is in the history books. Therefore we cannot expect history to yield accurate information about the past.

Lyotard was a promoter of deconstructionism, the drive to take apart, or deconstruct, all metanarratives. Lyotard and others of his persuasion believe in the destruction of any objective knowledge of reality, morality, literature or anything else.

The suspicion that Freud directed at individuals' motives, postmodernism now directs at culture as a whole. We saw earlier that we can describe postmodernism as minus faith and minus reason (– F – R = postmodernism). Postmodernism represents the end of the line: there is no objective faith and no objective knowledge of reality (reason, values or anything else).

*A **postmodern litany**.* Following is a sample of the "truths" that some postmodernists affirm—and they are surprisingly sure of them, considering that they also claim there is no objective truth:

• There is no such thing as an objective view of reality. We are shaped by our culture. We can have "objectivity" within our own cultural standards, but we can never have transcultural or supracultural objectivity.

- Because our outlook is culturally determined, we cannot judge another culture.

- There are no facts, only interpretations (Friedrich Nietzsche).

- History is fiction. History is written from the bias of the writer's culture, race or gender. What is called "historic" is wholly subjective (Michel Foucault).

- Knowledge is power. We must be suspicious of anyone who claims to give us truth. They are only out to further their own (and their group's) vested interests (Michel Foucault).

- Ethical claims are mere sentiment. We cannot call anything right or wrong. For example, there are no neutral grounds on which to condemn the Holocaust (Richard Rorty).

- Deconstruction is justice. We must ferret out the contradictions in every piece of literature so that we can uphold justice and avoid injustice (Jacques Derrida).

- Whoever "spins" best wins. Since there is no objective truth, all we have is rhetoric. Whoever plays the game best wins; make sure it is you (Stanley Fish).

Concrete in the hole. The following analogy of a tree helps illustrate the radical nature of postmodernists' claims.

The tree represents faith and reason (F + R) in full flower. Some philosophical views hack off branches (discard certain arguments). Others might shrink the tree (reason is of some value, but not very much). Still others chop the tree off at the trunk (no apologetic is allowed). Other views would dig up the roots (critique all foundational assumptions). Postmodernism takes the final step of pouring concrete into the hole so that nothing will ever grow there again.

Lewis agrees. As a Christian believer at the center of classic Christian doctrine, C. S. Lewis would clash with many aspects of postmodernism. Christianity claims that God has spoken in understandable terms to human beings in real history and that God even entered human history in Jesus Christ, God incarnate. However, there are certain points that C. S. Lewis would likely agree with postmodern philosophers.

1. There are limits to knowledge. We cannot arrive at a comprehensive knowledge of reality through reason alone. Lewis held that "reality is very odd" and that ultimate truth "must have the character-

istic of strangeness."[1] Lewis criticized the arrogance and pretensions of modernism.

2. Your perspective does affect what you see. In an essay titled "Meditation on a Tool Shed," Lewis describes the experience of entering a tool shed and observing a shaft of sunlight coming through a hole in the roof. He could see the gradually widening beam of light with specks of dust floating downward. He calls this initial view "looking at" the beam. However, there is another perspective that involves "looking along" the beam.[2] In order to do that, you would need to go to the beam and look outside through the crack. Then you could see trees, clouds and sun. "Looking at" or analyzing has become the preferred means of "knowing," and it can be valid as far as it goes. But there is much more to life. In fact, sometimes it is impossible to "look at" and "look along" at the same time. For instance, you cannot both be fully engaged in a romantic relationship and analyze it at the same moment, because analysis involves a distancing from the intimate engagement. So your perspective determines what you see, and each perspective does not necessarily allow all that can be seen.

3. Our perspective affects the way we view history. In *The Discarded Image* Lewis discusses the medieval worldview. He concludes that it is splendid and coherent; the only problem is that it is not true. Historical models can help us to get at reality, but they do not exhaustively describe it. He writes:

No model is a catalogue of ultimate realities, and none is mere fantasy. . . . [E]ach reflects the prevalent psychology of an age almost as much as it reflects the state of that age's knowledge. It is not impossible that our own model will die a violent death. . . . [A] good cross-examiner can do wonders. He will not elicit falsehoods from an honest witness. But in relation to the total truth in the witness's mind, the structure of examination is like a stencil. It determines how much of the total truth will appear and what pattern it will suggest.[3]

In his Cambridge inaugural address, Lewis argued that the Renaissance did not happen; or if it did happen, it did not happen in England. He thought other descriptions were more helpful in getting at the historical shifts that took place at that time. (Likewise at some point we may find a better name than postmodernism for the view now prevalent.) Lewis said, "All lines of demarcation between what we call periods should be subject to constant revision. . . . Unlike dates, periods are not facts. . . . Change is never complete and change never ceases. Nothing is ever quite new. . . . All divisions will falsify material to some extent; the best one can do is to choose those which will falsify it least."[4]

4. Our ideas of God and reality are too small. Sometimes our cherished ideas need to be smashed so we can gain a better and more accurate view of reality. What I need is not my idea of my wife, but my wife. What I need is not my idea of my sons, but my sons. And of course what we all need most is not our own pet theories about God, but God himself. As J. B. Phillips titled one of his books, *Your God Is Too Small.* Lewis said, "My idea of God is not a divine idea. It has to be shattered time after time. He shatters it Himself. He is the great Iconoclast." In fact, Lewis maintained, "All reality is Iconoclastic."[5]

5. Culture can blind us to some aspects of who we are. In chapter three, on chronological snobbery, we saw Lewis defend our need for old books to help correct our restricted viewpoints. (I would add that interactions with other cultures help as well.) Lewis said that we need to let the breezes of the centuries blow through our minds, cleansing

us of the culturally induced distortions in our perspective.[6]

Lewis disagrees. While we have seen several ways in which Lewis would agree with the postmodernist view, he would also voice major disagreements, particularly to the claim that we can have no objective knowledge of truth or morality. If Lewis were with us today, here is what he might say: The most basic postmodern contentions are self-refuting. Lewis would ask, "Is it objectively true to say that there are no objective truths? Can you deny the validity of reason without using reason?" If all perspectives of reality are culturally determined, then that statement itself is culturally determined; or is it somehow transcultural? If all metanarratives are suspect because they are oppressive, then is not postmodernism also a metanarrative and equally suspect? If all knowledge claims are a grab for power, then are not the contentions of postmodernism equally motivated by the drive for power?

Are postmodernists "sawing off the branch they are sitting on," as Lewis said Freud and Marx were doing? It is fascinating that one postmodern writer picks up this image and says yes, he is sawing off the branch, but there is no ground to fall onto.[7]

Suspicion can work both ways. Postmodernists would do well to suspect their own suspicions. In "Bulverism," the essay quoted in chapter nine on wish fulfillment, Lewis argues that the psychological charge "Christianity is a crutch" can be answered by the counter charge "Atheism is a crutch." In a similar way, postmodernism (to echo Marx) is an opiate of the conscience or (to echo Freud) is a grand Oedipus complex wishing the death of the heavenly Father.

Postmodernism's moral conclusions deserve suspicion. A view which maintains that there are no grounds on which we can condemn the Holocaust deserves suspicion. Some radical feminists who are not Christians maintain that moral relativism actually perpetuates

oppression and injustice to women because it makes the terms *justice*
and *injustice* merely emotive statements.[8]

The view that cultures differ so widely that there is no common
moral ground is false. In "The Poison of Subjectivism" Lewis says that
this belief

> is a lie, a good resounding lie. If a man will go into a library and
> spend a few days with the *Encyclopedia of Religion and Ethics,* he
> will soon discover the massive unanimity of the practical reason
> in man. From the Babylonian Hymn to Samos, from the laws of
> Manu, the Book of the Dead, the Analects, the Stoics, the Pla-
> tonists, from Australian aborigines and Redskins, he will collect
> the same triumphantly monotonous denunciations of oppres-
> sion, murder, treachery and falsehood; the same injunctions of
> kindness to the aged, the young, and the weak, of almsgiving
> and impartiality and honesty.[9]

Lewis debunked the notion that cultures do not share any common concept of morality: "But the pretense that we are presented
with a mere chaos—as though no outline of universally accepted
value shows through—is simply false and should be contradicted in
season and out of season wherever it is met."[10] Derek Freeman attempts to contradict the lie in his book *Margaret Mead and Samoa.*
Freeman raises profound questions about the shoddy scholarship
and dishonesty of Mead, the patron saint and popularizer of cultural
relativism—which became the foundational assumption of postmodernism.

We should oppose the manner in which deconstructionists approach an author's text. One postmodern professor sought to destroy
his students' love of literature by taking the view of one who stands
above and over texts, "interrogating" them, reading between the

lines, and reading against the grain. Postmodern critics raise deep suspicions of the supposedly racist, sexist, ethnocentric motives of the authors whom they "interrogate." While the Bible tells us that "perfect love drives out fear" (1 John 4:18), postmodernists display "a perfect fear that drives out love." By contrast, Lewis urges us to "receive" literature—"Look. Listen. Receive. Get yourself out of the way." Lewis loved imaginative writing and said, "My own eyes are not enough for me, I will see through those of others."[11]

There is a profound connection between literature and love. When we read a story with the right attitude, we "get out" of ourselves and "get into" the writer's perspective. Lewis says, "In the moral sphere, every act of justice or charity involves putting ourselves in the other person's place, and thus transcending our own competitive particularity. In coming to understand anything, we are rejecting the facts as they are for us. Yet, the primary impulse of each of us is to aggrandize himself." The cure, Lewis says, is love. "In love we escape from our self into one another." Here is a more perfect love that casts out fear.[12]

The partial exaggerated to the whole. I believe Lewis would point out that the claims of postmodernism are partial truths exaggerated into the whole truth. Postmodernists exaggerate the difficulty of objectivity, they exaggerate the imprecision of interpretation, and they exaggerate the impossibilities of crosscultural communication. Certainly the claim to absolutes can become oppressive, but the denial of absolutes leads to even greater oppression. In *The Abolition of Man*, Lewis argues that we have already seen the fruit of moral relativism. He points out that no relativist has ever been given power and used it for benevolent ends.[13]

Above all, Lewis would caution us not to build our worldview on a passing mood or trend such as postmodernism. He says, "If you take your stand on the prevalent view, how long do you suppose it will prevail. . . . All you can say about my taste is that it is old-fashioned; yours will soon be the same."[14]

DIFFERENT CULTURES, DIFFERENT MORALS?

Damon waves a hand and says, "Wait a minute, wait a minute. It sounds like you have to be either stuck in cement or floating in space somewhere."

"Nice analogy—I think. What do you mean?" Brenda asks.

"Well, I can't buy the postmodern idea that we have to mistrust everything that's written as history." Damon gestures at the long bookshelves that stretch away from the corner of the store where the group meets. "If you read every book that's here, I'm sure you'll find a lot of garbage, but I can't see being suspicious of every single fact you read. For one thing, it's too exhausting. But it's obvious to me that morals are relative. Different cultures have different ideas of right and wrong."

Lenae points out, "I think I'd agree, but C. S. Lewis didn't think so."

"OK, but he didn't have access to the intercultural communication and interaction we have now. In his day, people in Africa or South America or Asia were considered savages."

"They were savages with morals," Mike points out.

"Their own morals," Damon returns. "Don't you think Lewis would have been shocked by some of the things those people did, if he'd had the chance to live and interact with them?"

The group looks toward John for an answer, and John hesitates before he says, "It's true, Lewis never went and lived in a radically different culture, but I think he had a profound understanding of human nature."

Julia says, "Each of us determines right and wrong for ourselves. If people in other parts of the world happen to arrive at the same guidelines as mine, doesn't that simply show that we're all part of the whole?"

Brenda turns to Julia and says rather sharply, "But what happens when it's the people right next door to you, and they have very different guide-

lines?" She looks at John and explains, "My daughter is friends with a girl in our neighborhood whose parents are . . . well, I don't consider myself narrow-minded, but their values clash with ours. It's becoming a real problem. I don't want to tell my daughter she can't go to this girl's house, but . . . well, I'm taking us off the subject. Sorry."

"Don't be sorry, and it's not really off the subject," John assures Brenda. "This is the kind of dilemma we get into when ideas of right and wrong really matter to us."

"So that proves it's all relative," declares Simon. "Brenda's family and her neighbor's family have developed different sets of rules because of their environment and circumstances or . . . well, for whatever reason."

Lenae asks, "OK, what would Mr. Lewis tell Brenda to do about her daughter?"

John says, "Now there's a practical question! We can talk for days about moral relativism in the abstract, but what do we do when it's right in our face? How about if we think about that this week and get into it at our next meeting?"

RELATIVISM

Aren't Morals Relative?

The following week the members of the Lewis study group are not so punctual as before. They straggle in one by one. Some are a little late. John wants to write it off to busy schedules, but he is sure that the topic of moral relativism is probing some sore points. He tells himself to relax: After all, we aren't discussing what I think; we're discussing what C. S. Lewis thought. I'll let him carry the ball . . . through his writings, of course. But I sure wish he was here. He'd do this a lot better than I can!

The group members greet each other but are rather subdued tonight. No one has anything special to say, not even Brenda. So John begins, "According to recent polls, more than two-thirds of Americans deny any belief in absolutes. Do you think they've considered the implications?" No one responds right away, so John continues, "If there are no absolutes, then we can't say that anything is really—that is, absolutely—evil. Think of Hitler and Stalin, the killing fields of Cambodia, ethnic cleansing in Bosnia, the stealing of food from starving people in Somalia, the terrorist attacks on innocent civilians on September 11, 2001, and the crime in our streets every day. Can we look at these events and honestly say there is no evil?"

Impatiently Simon responds, "Some things are so manifestly evil, there's no argument. Nobody in their right mind would say those things are good."

Lenae objects, "The terrorists thought it was good. Crime is good if you're a criminal. Hitler believed in what he was doing. Who's to say they're wrong? I mean, I'm not sure if I believe that, but that's what I've heard people say."

"Exactly! Who's to say they're wrong?" Damon asks. He repeats with emphasis, "Who's to say? That's the question. Who makes the rules?"

Julia replies, "I can't make the rules for you, and you can't make the rules for me. And Brenda . . . well, you can make the rules for your daughter, but you can't make the rules for your daughter's friend."

"Even when she's teaching my daughter to lie and steal?" Brenda demands. Silence greets her question.

After a moment John says, "As an atheist, C. S. Lewis denied that there were any moral absolutes. When he became a Christian, he insisted that Christian morality had to go beyond personal opinion. It had to fit with life as a whole, or it was meaningless. The question is, are there moral standards that are written into the universe?"

PROBLEMS WITH RELATIVISM

The crooked line. Lewis came to question moral relativism as a result of one of his own objections to faith—the problem of evil. The classic argument against God went like this: If God were all-powerful, he could eliminate evil. If he were all-good, he would eliminate evil. There is evil; therefore there must not be an all-good, all-powerful God.

Despite the apparent strength of this argument, Lewis gradually saw an inconsistency in his own position. If there were no God, then there would be no solid basis to say that anything was good or evil. Then where had he gotten his idea of evil? He wrote:

> But how had I got this idea of just and unjust? A man does not call a line crooked unless he has some idea of a straight line. What was I comparing this universe with when I called it un-just? If the whole show was bad and senseless from A to Z, so to speak, why did I, who was supposed to be part of the show, find myself in such violent reaction against it? A man feels wet when he falls into water because man is not a water animal: a fish would not feel wet. Of course I could have given up my idea of justice by saying it was nothing but a private idea of my own. But if I did that, my argument against God collapsed too—for the argument depended on saying that the world was really unjust, not simply that it did not happen to please my private fancies. Thus in trying to prove that God did not exist—in other words, that the whole of reality is senseless—I was forced to assume that one part of reality—namely my idea of justice was full of sense. Consequently, atheism turns out to be too simple.[1]

If there is evil, Lewis concluded, there must be a fixed, absolute, infinite, transcendent standard by which we can judge it to be evil. This absolute standard of good suggests a God who is the infinite reference point.

Proud of being a double-crosser? Lewis also took note of how people assume a fixed set of morals in their ordinary interactions in life. Though they might deny any absolute standard, they constantly appeal to a standard of fairness when they say, "Come on, you promised," "That's my seat, I was there first," "Why should you shove in first?" and so on. People regularly appeal to fixed standards of behavior in families, marriages, schools, community and political life. Rarely do you hear people say about such things, "To hell with your standard."[2] More often they deny they are violating the standard, or they give an excuse for why it is all right to do so this time.

Lewis shows the ridiculousness of the idea that there could exist a society with a radically divergent morality, where our good is regarded as evil and our evil is regarded as good. He speculates on what such a society would look like:

> Think of a country where people were admired for running away in battle, or where a man felt proud of double-crossing all the people who had been kindest to him. You might just as well try to imagine a country where two and two made five. Men have differed as regards what people you ought to be unselfish to—whether it was only your own family, or your fellow countrymen, or everyone. But they have always agreed that you ought not to put yourself first. Selfishness has never been admired. Men have differed as to whether you should have one wife or four. But they have always agreed that you must not simply have any woman you liked.[3]

Eventually Lewis went to great lengths to document the universality and timelessness of moral standards. In the appendix to *The Abolition of Man* he cites the almost monotonously similar moral standards of ancient Egyptians, Babylonians, Hindus, Chinese, Greeks, Romans and others.[4] Though the specifics may differ, the general outline is the same throughout all cultures.

TRUTH OR TASTE?

Since it is impossible to deny that all people everywhere recognize moral standards, relativists are forced to take a different tack, which on the surface appears broad-minded and generous. They relegate morals to the area of personal feeling. Just as we might say, "You can choose any soda pop or shoe style or house paint color which feels right to you, and I can choose any that feels right to me," the moral relativist says, "You can have whatever religion or morality works for you, and I can have another one that works just as well for me." This expansive approach wipes out the idea that there is objective truth in ethics or religion. Religious or ethical opinions become matters of personal taste. Truth does not matter (or else is unknowable); only subjective feelings matter.

Lewis counters the emotive approach to moral issues in *The Abolition of Man*. He starts by surveying a sample textbook he received in the mail, in which the authors reduce a value judgment to mere sentiment. They claim that the statement "the waterfall is sublime" only appears to say something important, when in reality the assertion only says something about the speaker's own feelings.[5]

The distinction may not seem critical when we are dealing with aesthetic judgments. After all, is beauty not in the eye of the beholder? But are we willing to assume that all statements about truth, goodness and beauty are only a matter of personal feeling? In other words, can we assume that there is nothing intrinsically good, and nothing that can with certainty be called beautiful, beyond our own sentiment?

The devaluing of feelings. The reduction of moral and religious values to a matter of feelings is so prevalent that we may not even notice it, let alone consider whether it is right. The idea was perhaps assumed, although never explicitly argued, in our education. G. K. Chesterton said "Education is implication." We often learn not what is explicitly taught but what is implied in what is said. Lewis explained how the indoctrination happens: "It is not a theory they put into his [a student's] mind but an assumption, which ten years hence, its origin forgotten and its presence unconscious, will condition him to take one side in a controversy which he has never recognized as a controversy at all."[6]

People are easily drawn to the emotive approach to ethics, perhaps because they want to be tolerant of others or because they want to honor other people's feelings. Ultimately, however, the approach devalues human feelings. Feelings are trivialized by the claim that, while values seem to be important, they are merely a matter of feelings.

Education of the affections. By contrast, classical education places a high value on feeling strongly about what is genuinely right or wrong. Lewis stands in the stream of classicists from antiquity when he says that true education is not only of the mind but also of the affections: "For every pupil who needs to be guarded from a weak excess of sensibility, there are three who need to be awakened from the slumber of cold vulgarity. The task of the modern educator is not to cut down jungles but to irrigate deserts. The right defense against false sentiments is to inculcate just sentiments."[7]

Aristotle held that the aim of education was to make the pupil like and dislike what he or she ought to like and dislike. In *The Republic* Plato states that the student is to be encouraged to hate the ugly and to give praise to beauty. For Plato the head is to rule the belly through "the chest;" that is, reason must rule sentiment through a passion for truth (perhaps a rightly informed conscience).

Lewis concluded that modern culture has produced people "without chests"—without a passion for good and a hatred for evil. "In a sort of ghastly simplicity, we remove the organ and demand the function. We make men without chests and expect of them virtue and enterprise. We laugh at honor and are shocked to find traitors in our midst. We castrate and bid the geldings be fruitful."[8]

HOPELESS INCONSISTENCY

The view that "morals are relative" not only ignores the universality of moral standards and trivializes human feelings, it turns out to be a philosophical position that is hopelessly inconsistent. In the sterility of the classroom a teacher may say that right and wrong are relative, but those same relativists often declaim loudly about the latest social issue and try to persuade others of their views, even scoffing at those who disagree.

Since moral relativists must avoid the embarrassing words *good* and *evil,* they often substitute less precise, fuzzier terms. In *The Abolition of Man* Lewis exposes such dishonesty:

> To abstain from calling it good and to use such predicates as "necessary," "progressive" or "efficient" would be a subterfuge. They could be forced in debate to answer the questions "necessary for what?" In the last resort they would have to admit that some state of affairs is good for its own sake. . . . Their skepticism about values is on the surface: it is for other people's values; about values current in their own set they are not nearly skeptical enough. . . . A great many of those who "debunk" traditional or (as they would say) "sentimental" values have in the background values of their own which they believe to be immune from the debunking process.[9]

To preserve society. But does an ethic based on preserving society have some merit after all? At least it goes beyond mere personal sentiment and reaches out to embrace the best interests of society at large. It avoids the clash of religious values by remaining nontheological. It does not depend on God or belief in God; instead it inquires "What will preserve society?" and then attempts to persuade a majority of the society's citizens to agree on appropriate laws to regulate community life.

For example, we could argue that murder is destructive to society because if murder is allowed, society will fall apart and ultimately be destroyed. Therefore murder should be outlawed so society can be preserved.

The flaw in this position is that it assumes that the preservation of society is an absolute value. What if we question that assumption? Why should this society be preserved? Others may desire—they may even actively seek—the society's destruction. On what grounds can such destruction be called evil? If there is no external, absolute standard to judge competing claims, who are we—who is anyone—to say which side is right? And if the problem is beyond discussion, what solution is left except guns and bombs?

In *The Abolition of Man* C. S. Lewis points out the principal reason that the good-of-society ethic can never work. He argues:

> From propositions about fact no *practical* conclusion can ever be drawn. *This will preserve society* cannot lead to *do this* except by the mediation of *society ought to be preserved*. *This will cost you your life* cannot lead directly to *do not do this:* it can lead to it only through felt desire or an acknowledged duty of self-preservation. The Innovator is trying to get a conclusion in the imperative mood out of premises in the indicative mood: and though he continues trying to all eternity, he cannot succeed, for the thing is impossible.[10]

In other words, you cannot get *ought* out of *is*. You cannot get "society ought to be preserved" from "society will be preserved." If the terrorist wants to murder, how can we say no? We can only say, "Says us" (the majority in the society). If the majority inexplicably decided that murder was good for society, then it would become right. The attempt to ground ethics on the good of society falls victim to what one author calls "the grand Sez Who?"[11]

THE IMPOTENCE OF RELATIVISM

To their credit, many relativists aim to bring about a better world. They want to eliminate racism and oppression and injustice; they want character, virtue, and decency. But what is the price of those admirable qualities? It is submission to an external moral standard by which we know those qualities are admirable.

In his book *The Death of Character* James Hunter says it clearly:

> We say we want a renewal of character in our day but we do not really know what to ask for. To have a renewal of character is to have a renewal of a creedal order that constrains, limits, binds, obligates and compels. This price is too high for us to pay. We want character without conviction; we want strong morality but without the emotional burden of guilt or shame; we want virtue but without particular moral justifications that invariably offend; we want good without having to name evil; we want decency without the authority to insist upon it; we want moral community without any limitations to personal freedom. In short, we want what we cannot possibly have on the terms that we want it.[12]

THE DARK SIDE OF RELATIVISM

In the final chapter of *The Abolition of Man* Lewis points out that since relativism has no reference point for ultimate good, those in society he names the "conditioners" shape the conscience of their followers to fit their own purposes. Without external moral standards, the effort goes disastrously wrong.

I have been told that Adolf Hitler kept a copy of Nietzche's *Thus Sprach Zarathustra* on his bedside table and gave a full set of Nietzsche's works to Mussolini as a gift. In Nietzschean philosophy the only goal is to exert the will to power. In a speech to the Hitler youth in Nuremberg, Hitler stated, "I desire to create a generation without conscience, imperious, relentless and cruel." Hitler's call for a super race was an echo of Nietzsche's "Übermensch" (superman). He felt that he could condition the human conscience in any way he wanted since he was not limited by any absolute standard of morality.

Benito Mussolini, the Italian dictator, also espoused relativism. He wrote, "Everything that I have said and done in these last years is relativism by intuition. . . . If relativism signifies contempt for fixed categories and men who claim to be bearers of an objective, immortal truth . . . then there is nothing more relativistic than fascistic attitudes and activity. . . . From the fact that all ideologies are mere fictions, the modern relativist infers that everybody has the right to create for himself his own ideology and to attempt to enforce it with all the energy of which he is capable."[13]

James Miller's fascinating biography *The Passion of Michel Foucault* points out the dark side of this founder of postmodernism (although Miller was sympathetic with Foucault's philosophy). Miller writes that Foucault wanted to destroy everything that is claimed to be "right" in Western culture, to maintain that there are no limits, no divisions, no boundaries between good and evil, reason and unreason, subject and object. One of his mottos was "Be Cruel," and he sometimes dwelled at length on images of cruelty in his writings. He practiced sadomasochism and anonymous gay sex in San Francisco bathhouses. Foucault often focused on the "limit experience"—death. Miller notes that Foucault's destruction of morality extends to "nearly everything that passes for right among a great many of America's left wing academics."[14]

Many of Foucault's American followers prefer to put a more attractive face on his philosophy. Miller writes:

> Most of these latter day Foucaultians are high-minded democrats; they are committed to forging a more diverse society in which whites and people of color, straights and gays, men and women, their various ethnic and gender differences intact, can nevertheless all live in compassionate harmony—an appealing if difficult goal, with deep roots in the Judeo-Christian tradition.[15]

As part of my doctoral program I took a class in Marxism from a Marxist. Karl Marx had an admirable vision of a utopian community of workers, but the reality of Marxism has been far different. Since Marx's view included no God and labeled religion as the "opiate" of the people, the outworking of Marxism had to destroy all religious belief.

The woman professor in our class was brilliant, articulate and gracious. She was a very good teacher, adept at answering questions and effective at countering serious challenges to her position. She was very good at articulating the injustices in society—sometimes practiced by religious people. However, toward the end of the semester, she came to a section on "strategy and tactics." It became clear to the students that for our professor there were no absolutes, that everything was relative to the goal to be achieved, and the ends justified the means. There was no intrinsic limit to prohibit the use of any tactic or strategy. Anyone was expendable in light of the larger good of the community—the masses of workers.

She did not lay this out explicitly, but when pressed with questions, this usually sure-footed professor became uncharacteristically unclear with her answers. When the class grasped the implications of what she was saying, the students at this secular university yelled at her. For the first time this unflappable professor was flustered and at a loss for words. She never did regain control of the class that day.

The Abolition of Man was published during World War II, when humanity had endured some of the worst consequences of moral relativism. Lewis foresaw much darker possibilities ahead: "I am doubtful whether history shows us one example of a man who, having stepped outside traditional morality and attained power, has used that power benevolently."[16]

LEWIS ON RELATIVISM

Here is what Lewis would have us learn and remember about moral relativism:

- If there is no absolute standard for good and evil (God), then there is no evil. One or the other has to go, either atheism or a major argument for atheism.

- If we equate value judgments with human feelings, we trivialize those feelings. True education involves cultivating a love for justice and a hatred for injustice. If we reduce values to feelings, we deprive ourselves of the passion we need to live by our moral commitments.

- The relativistic viewpoint is hopelessly inconsistent.

- The attempt to create an ethic without God is doomed to failure.

- No relativist who has been given absolute power has used that power benevolently.

FIRM, NOT FUZZY

Brenda is chewing her lower lip thinking. John lets her think, and no one else leaps in to fill the gap of silence. John wonders if they all recall Brenda's moral dilemma concerning her daughter. Finally Brenda says, "So Lewis would say it's not enough to just sit my daughter's friend down and tell her, 'I prefer that you don't teach my daughter to steal.' "

"So what's your alternative?" *Damon asks.*

"I can say, 'We don't do that in our family.' "

"And she'll say, 'In my family we do.' "

"Yes, and maybe that would be the end of it. I'll just have to keep them apart. But . . . no, it's more than that. It isn't right to take what doesn't belong to you. I can't just take all the children's books in this store and walk out without paying for them. Much as I'd like to!"

Julia asks, "But what keeps you from doing it? Isn't it the fear of getting caught?"

Hesitantly Brenda says, "No, it's because it would be wrong."

Simon points out, "It's wrong because if everybody did that, the store would go broke, and then we wouldn't have a bookstore here, and that would be wrong. So it goes back to what's best for society."

Brenda shakes her head. "I think it's more than that."

"Does your daughter know that stealing is wrong?" *Mike pointedly asks Brenda.*

"Of course she does! At least I hope so. I guess I never thought I had to tell her, because . . . well, I'm not sure what I mean."

John says, "Last week Lenae asked me what C. S. Lewis would tell Brenda to do about her situation. Lewis isn't here, so I'll do my best. I think he would say that Brenda and her daughter and her daughter's friend and all of us here know that stealing is wrong. It's part of that universal moral law. But he would also say that we—like all human beings—deliberately violate our own consciences. And he'd say that's where Christianity comes in."

Julia corrects him. "You mean that's where spirituality in general comes in."

"Maybe spirituality in general, yes, but Christianity in particular."

With a puzzled look Lenae asks, "But don't all religions teach the same thing?"

OTHER RELIGIONS

There Are So Many Religions, How Can You Say Which One Is Right?

John knows that Lenae's question, "Don't all religions teach the same thing?" is not so much a question as an assertion. He looks around at the group to see whether anyone will voice an opinion.

Julia speaks up. "All religions teach love and tolerance toward your fellow human beings. So at their center, they're all the same."

Simon barely conceals a smug expression. "Isn't it interesting that C. S. Lewis, the great Christian, would have to agree with that?"

John asks, "Why?"

"He believed that everybody in the world holds to the same ideas of right and wrong, good and evil. So he'd have to say that all religions believe the same thing. And if they all believe the same thing, they must all be right. Except of course I believe they're all wrong."

Brenda says, "Fundamentalist Christians think they're the only ones who are right. They came around our neighborhood passing out pamphlets that said 'Jesus Christ—the Only Way to God.' I was so turned off."

Mike comments, "You live in an interesting neighborhood. Did they give one to your neighbor who steals?"

"Religions aren't all the same," Damon objects. "Otherwise why would people kill Muslims just because they're Muslims, or Christians just because they're Christians? Somebody thinks they're different, and that the difference matters."

Julia has an answer. "People who kill in the name of religion can't be true adherents of their religion. Otherwise they'd recognize the unity and oneness in all faiths."

Quickly Lenae says, "Right! All religions teach tolerance and understanding. You can't stand in judgment of somebody else's religion."

John says, "OK, it sounds like we've got two questions going. First, are all religions really the same, or is there a difference? And two, how can we say which one—if any—is the right one?"

Brenda says, "I doubt if C. S. Lewis will be much help. Once he turned to Christianity, he must have written off all the other religions."

John replies, "Actually, Lewis felt it was atheism that wrote off all religious claims as false, while he was free to affirm truth wherever it was found."

"So he did accept the truth of other religions!" Julia says triumphantly.

"It might be more precise to say he accepted truths in other religions. By that I mean he recognized the similarities—as well as the significant differences—between religions."

Simon asks, "OK, so what are the similarities and differences? According to Lewis, I mean?"

THE ONLY STREAM

In *The Silver Chair,* the sixth of the Narnia chronicles, Jill is stranded in a forest alone and is very thirsty. She hears the sound of running water and finds a stream. But then she sees that there is a lion sitting

by the stream. She is too thirsty to run away. The Lion speaks to her:
"If you are thirsty, you may drink." The voice is not like a man's but
"deeper, wilder, and stronger; a heavy golden voice."

"Are you not thirsty?" said the Lion.

"I'm dying of thirst," said Jill.

"Then drink," said the Lion.

"May I—could I—would you mind going away while I do?"
said Jill.

The Lion answered this only by a look and a very low growl.
And as Jill gazed at its motionless bulk, she realized that she
might as well have asked the whole mountain to move aside for
her convenience.

The delicious and rippling noise of the stream was driving her
nearly frantic.

"Will you promise not to—do anything to me if I come?" said
Jill.

"I make no promise," said the Lion.

Jill was so thirsty now that, without noticing it, she had come a
step nearer.

"Do you eat girls?" she said.

"I have swallowed up girls and boys, women and men, kings
and emperors, cities and realms," said the Lion. It didn't say this
as if it were boasting, nor as if it were sorry, nor as if it were angry. It just said it.

"I daren't come and drink," said Jill.

"Then you will die of thirst," said the Lion.

"Oh dear!" said Jill, coming another step nearer. "I suppose I must go and look for another stream then."

"There is no other stream," said the Lion.[1]

NARROW-MINDED?

Christians through the ages have maintained that there is "no other stream," no other way to salvation, besides Jesus Christ. So it is not surprising that one of the most persistent objections to Christianity is: "How can you be so narrow-minded as to claim that Christ is the only way to God?" I have seen polls that identify this as the number one or number two objection of nonbelievers (along with the charge that the church is full of hypocrites).

In *Mere Christianity* C. S. Lewis asserts that a commitment to Christ does not necessitate the denial of truth in other religions. He writes, "If you are a Christian you do not have to believe that all the other religions are wrong all through. If you are an atheist, you do have to believe that the main point in all religions of the world is simply a huge mistake. If you are a Christian, you are free to think that all these religions, even the queerest ones, contain at least some hint of truth."[2]

So atheism turns out to be the most narrow-minded of all belief systems, because it denies the truth of the central principles of any and all religions. Atheists would insist that all religious people have at the core made a "huge mistake." On the other hand, Christians are free to unearth the truths found in all religions.

A GOOD DOSE OF REALITY

Major religions are bound to have at least some basis in truth. For an idea to gain wide acceptance, and especially to persist for centuries, it must contain a good dose of reality. Human beings, created by God and placed in God's world, have an innate sense of what rings true, although it is warped by sin. The further away from reality a religious viewpoint strays, the fewer adherents it gathers. Even the most bizarre cult can gain some followers; but the more fanciful its claims, the less credibility it has.

As I have studied many religious viewpoints and have made a special study of cults and new religious movements, I find certain points where I agree with them. For example, I can agree with Jews and Muslims that there is one infinite God distinct from creation. I can agree with Eastern and New Age followers about environmental concerns and the significance of imagination and creativity. I can find truth in each belief system without completely embracing any of them.

C. S. Lewis provides a way to map out the points of similarity between religions. In *The Problem of Pain* he writes of four different types of religious claims: (1) numinous, (2) moral, (3) combination of numinous and moral, and (4) incarnation. First is the claim to what Lewis calls the "numinous."[3]

The numinous. The numinous describes a sense of mystery in the face of a supernatural encounter. Rudolf Otto's classic book *The Idea of the Holy* uses the term *mysterium tremendum* for the same kind of experience. It is a sense of being in the presence of a mysterious force that makes us tremble with fear, and although we are afraid, at the same time we are drawn toward that which we fear. In the films *Close Encounters of the Third Kind* and *E.T. the Extra-Terrestrial,* the encounter with aliens is both fear-producing and fascinating, both awe-full and attracting. So also with divine encounters.

Why do you think so many people are fascinated with horror films? Some people absolutely love to be scared out of their wits by the prospect of meeting strange supernatural forces. I remember a woman at the Ligonier Valley Study Center who had a passionate love of horror movies. Yet she, as a mature adult, had a deathly fear of the short trek in relative darkness from our lecture house to the house where she was staying. Fed by images from the movies, she imagined all kinds of threats lurking there in the dark. She was easily scared, yet she also loved to be scared.

I saw the same ambivalence in my oldest son, Trey, when he was about three years old. I used to have a stack of children's books on the bed and we would read through several before bedtime. One of his favorites was *Where the Wild Things Are*. In the story a little boy is disciplined by being sent to bed without his supper. His room turns into a fantastic adventure in which he boards a ship and sails to "where the wild things are." I had read this story to Trey before, but one night when we reached the part where the wild things roar their terrible roars and show their terrible claws, he started to shake in my arms and said, "Daddy, stop!" So I stopped and started to read a new book. Trey said, "No Daddy, read this one" and pointed to *Where the Wild Things Are*. I picked it up and began to read again until I got to where the wild things are roaring, and again he began to shake and said, "Daddy, stop!" Again I stopped and started a new book. We stopped and started that way several times. Trey did not want to be scared by the monsters, and at the same time he did want to be scared.

As a literary illustration of the numinous, Lewis uses a passage from Kenneth Grahame's *The Wind in the Willows*. Rat and Mole are searching for Portly, a lost otter. They are guided to the sleeping otter by distant music, and to their surprise they find themselves in the presence of the god Pan. Mole speaks: " 'Rat,' he found breath to whisper, shaking, 'are you afraid?' 'Afraid?' murmured the Rat, his eyes shining with unutterable love. 'Afraid? Of Him? O, never, never. And yet—and yet, O Mole, I am afraid.' "[4]

Such ambivalence in the face of the holy or the supernatural other is common to all religions from animism to pantheism to theism (except for the strictly "moral"). Lewis says we can hold one of two positions about the universal human experience of awe: "Either it is a mere twist in the human mind, corresponding to nothing objective and serving no biological function, yet showing no tendency to disappear from that mind at its fullest development in poet, philosopher, or saint; or else, it is a direct experience of the really supernatural, to which the name Revelation might properly be given."[5]

The moral. The second religious claim is the moral. Some religions or philosophies have a sense of moral oughtness but downplay any encounter with the numinous or supernatural. Confucianism, Platonism and Stoicism place a strong emphasis on the moral but keep any religious encounter in the background. Lewis argues that this sense of moral oughtness is either rooted in reality or else is a human invention. In *The Abolition of Man* he calls the sense of oughtness the "belief that certain attitudes are really true, and others are really false."[6] As with the sense of awe, we have an either-or choice of how to explain morality: "Either we are rational spirit obliged forever to obey the absolute values of the Tao [universal moral law], or else we are mere nature to be kneaded and cut into new shapes for the pleasure of masters who must, by hypothesis, have no motive but their own natural impulses."[7]

The moral-numinous. The third religious claim is the combination of the numinous and the moral. Some religions emphasize the numinous over the moral; others stress the moral but downplay the numinous. The great theistic faiths—Christianity, Judaism and Islam—join the numinous and the moral. Thus you have the all-powerful,

awesome, holy God who condemns wrong. Here again we face an either-or: The combination of numinous and moral "may be madness—a madness congenital to man and oddly fortunate in its results—or it may be revelation."[8]

The incarnation. The fourth religious claim is incarnation, and
this is what sets Christianity apart as unique from all other religions
or philosophies. Christians can agree with animists on the numinous,
with Confucianists on the moral, and with Judaism and Islam on the
combination of numinous-moral. But the claim to incarnation—God
entered a specific historical place and time in Jesus Christ—is utterly
unique. It is also either true or false.

If the claim of incarnation is true, it is of ultimate significance. If
the claim is false, it deserves the rage that Muslims, Jews and Jeho-
vah's Witnesses direct toward it. Lewis points out that "Islam denies
the Incarnation. It will not allow that God has descended into flesh
or that manhood has been exalted into Deity."[9] To Muslims there is a
radical difference between Allah and material creation that cannot be
bridged.

THE FULFILLMENT OF ALL THREE

In the incarnation of Jesus Christ we see the fulfillment of the three
previous religious claims. In Christ the numinous becomes articulate. In Christ the moral is demonstrated in a perfect life. In Christ
we see justice, mercy and love in harmony as the numinous is guard-
ian of the moral.

The death of Christ solves the problem of how sinful human beings come into personal relationship with the awesome, transcendent, holy God. In a letter to Sheldon Vanauken, Lewis quotes Con-
fucius: " 'This is the Tao (moral law). I do not know anyone that has
kept it!' That's significant: One can really go directly from there to the

epistle of Romans."[10] If there is a moral law and no one has ever kept it, we must ask, "What can I do with my guilt?" To that question the death and resurrection of Christ provides the final and sufficient answer.

In *God in the Dock* Lewis shows the difficulty with the idea that Jesus was a great moral teacher but not God incarnate. Lewis points out that Christ made

> claims which if not true are those of a megalomaniac, compared with whom Hitler was the most sane and humble of men. There is no half-way house and there is no parallel in other religions. If you had gone to Buddha and asked him, "Are you the son of Brahma?" he would have said, "My son, you are still in the veil of illusion." If you had gone to Socrates and asked, 'Are you Zeus?' he would have laughed at you. If you had gone to Mohammed and asked, "Are you Allah?" he would have rent his clothes, then cut your head off. If you had asked Confucius, "Are you Heaven?" I think he would have probably replied, "Remarks which are not in accordance with nature are in bad taste." The idea of a great moral teacher saying what Christ said is out of the question. In my opinion, the only person who can say that sort of thing is either God or a complete lunatic suffering from that form of delusion which undermines the whole mind of man. If you think you are a poached egg, when you are looking for a piece of toast to suit, you may be sane, but if you think you are God, there is no chance for you. We may note in passing that He was never regarded as a mere moral teacher. He did not produce that kind of effect on any of the people who actually met Him. He produced mainly three effects—Hatred—Terror—Adoration. There was no trace of people expressing mild approval.[11]

Either Christ is God incarnate or he is not. If he made such an outrageous claim—which he did—then he is a liar, he is a lunatic or he is Lord. The claim that God became incarnate as a man in history sets Christianity apart from all others and leads to the "all or nothing" claims which Christians boldly make.

THICK OR CLEAR?

Lewis used the interesting metaphor of classifying religions as we do soups, into "thick" and "clear." A thick beef stew is rich and dark with lots of meat and vegetables. "Thick" religions have blood and sacrifice, ritual and ecstatic rites. A chicken consommé is clear. "Clear" religions are based on ethical and philosophical principles. Lewis gives us examples: "By Thick I mean those which have orgies and ecstasies and local attachments: Africa is full of thick religions. By Clear I mean those which are philosophically, ethically and universalizing: Stoicism, Buddhism, and the Ethical Church are clear religions."[12]

Lewis goes on to argue that the true religion must be the right combination of thick and clear because God has made all kinds of people: the child and the adult, the uneducated and the educated, the heart and the head. If the true religion were only thick, it would give us no clear principles of morality or answers to our deep spiritual questions, and it would be impossible to know that it was the one true way except by intuition or passion alone—an inadequate measure of truth. On the other hand, if the true religion were only clear, it could be known philosophically and ethically but would be inaccessible to the uneducated and to primitive people. There is much in the world that is mysterious, earthy, romantic and beyond reason. Lewis wrote: "Now if there is a true religion it must be both Thick and Clear for the true God must have made both the child and the man, both the savage and the citizen, both the head and the belly."[13]

Sometimes people stumble at the language of "blood" and "sacrifice" in Christian theology. It seems so primitive and earthy. This thick aspect of Christian faith is similar to other religious perspectives. A believer could observe a tribe somewhere sacrificing a chicken to ward off evil spirits and say, "You know, I don't believe everything they believe, but I do agree that sacrifice is necessary to deal with evil." Jesus' death on the cross is certainly a thick aspect of Christianity.

CHRISTIANITY OR HINDUISM?

Lewis argued that only two religions satisfy the criteria of being both thick and clear—Hinduism and Christianity. When Lewis first struggled with various religious options, he seriously considered Hinduism. In *Surprised by Joy* he wrote:

> The question was no longer to find the one simply true religion among a thousand religions simply false. It was rather, 'Where has religion reached its true maturity? Where, if anywhere, have all the hints of all Paganism been fulfilled?'. . . . There were really only two answers possible: either in Hinduism or in Christianity. . . . Whatever you could find elsewhere you could find better in one of these. But Hinduism seemed to have two disqualifications. For one thing, it appeared to be not so much a moralized and philosophical maturity of Paganism as a mere oil-and-water coexistence of philosophy side by side with Paganism unpurged; the Brahmin meditating in the forest, and, in the village a few miles away, temple prostitution, sati, cruelty, monstrosity. And secondly, there was no historical claim as in Christianity.[14]

Lewis offers other hints as to why he rejected Hinduism. In a letter he says, "Your Hindus certainly sound delightful. But what do they deny? That has always been my trouble . . . to find any proposition that they would pronounce false. But truth must surely involve exclusions."[15] Lewis alluded to the pantheistic principle of nondistinction, that there is ultimately no difference between you and me, between me and a tree, between true and false or between good and evil. Many quotes from Hindu and Buddhist writers demonstrate this concept.[16] Lewis says, "Confronted with a cancer or a slum, the Pantheist can say, 'If you could only see it from the divine point of view, you would realize that this also is God.' The Christian replies, 'Don't talk damned nonsense.' "[17] Experience and common sense tell us that good and bad are not the same. A person who disallows all differences is out of touch with reality.

WHAT ABOUT THOSE WHO DON'T HEAR?

But if Christianity is the one true religion, the only one with the right mixture of thick and clear, the only one which acknowledges that God has come to earth in the flesh, then what happens to those who never have the privilege of hearing about it? The question is an agonizing one for Christians and a point of attack for non-Christians. Lewis did not shy away from it, although his view is controversial.

In the final book of the Narnia chronicles, *The Last Battle,* an ape named Shift starts a false religion by dressing up a donkey in a lion skin to impersonate Aslan. The enemies of Narnia are the Calormene, who worship the god Tash. Tash demands human sacrifice and other evil practices. Shift claims (with Aslan's presumed endorsement) that Tash and Aslan are one. He calls the new god Tashlan. There is a young Calormene soldier named Emeth (Hebrew for truth) who believes in Tash but concentrates on Tash's awesomeness rather than his cruelty. Shift claims that Tash is in a certain building. Emeth desperately wants to know what Tash is really like, so he courageously in-

sists on entering the building and is killed. Toward the end of the
book, Emeth wanders in the afterlife happy but dazed. Aslan comes
to meet Emeth. Emeth says:

> I fell at his feet and thought this is the hour of death, for the
> Lion (who is worthy of all honour) will know that I have served
> Tash all my days and not him. Nevertheless it is better to see the
> Lion and die than to be Tisroc of the whole world and live and
> not have seen him. But the Glorious One bent down his golden
> head and touched my forehead with his tongue and said, "Son,
> thou art welcome." But I said, "Alas, Lord, I am no son of thine
> but a servant of Tash." He answered, "Child, all the service thou
> hast done to Tash, I account as service done to me." Then by
> reason of my great desire for wisdom and understanding, I
> overcame my fear and questioned the Glorious One and said,
> "Lord, is it then true, as the ape said, that thou and Tash are
> one?" The Lion growled so that the earth shook (but his wrath
> was not against me) and said, "It is false. Not because he and I
> are one, but because we are opposites, I take to me the services
> which thou has done to him for he and I are of such different
> kinds that no service which is vile can be done for me and none
> which is not vile can be done to him. Therefore, if any man
> swears by Tash and keeps his oath for the oath's sake, it is by me
> that he has truly sworn, though he knows it not and it is I who
> rewards him. And if any man does cruelty in my name, then
> though he says the name of Aslan, it is Tash whom he serves,
> and by Tash his deed is accepted. Dost thou understand child?"
> I said, "Lord, thou knowest how much I understand." But I said
> also (for the truth constrained me), "yet I have been seeking
> Tash all my days." "Beloved," said the Glorious One, "unless thy

desire had been for me thou wouldst not have sought so long and so true. For all find what they truly seek."[18]

Many people have puzzled over this passage by Lewis. I have been asked about it many times. Is there another way of salvation other than belief in Jesus? Is this only fiction and not in line with C. S. Lewis's views? It does appear that Lewis was what is called "inclusivist." An inclusivist believes that the only way to be saved is through Christ, but a person does not necessarily need a conscious knowledge of Christ in order to be saved. An "exclusivist" believes that Christ is the only way to be saved, and a person needs a conscious knowledge of Christ. Although Lewis was apparently an "inclusivist," he was definitely not a "universalist" who believes that everybody is saved.

We find other evidence that Lewis was an inclusivist in a letter he wrote:

I think that every prayer which is sincerely made even to a false god or to a very imperfectly conceived true God is accepted by the true God; and that Christ saves many who do not think they know Him, for He is (dimly) present in the *good* side of the inferior teachers whom they follow. In the parable of the Sheep and the Goats (Matthew XXV.31 and following) those who are saved do not seem to know that they have served Christ. But, of course, our anxiety about unbelievers is most usefully employed when it leads us not to speculation but to earnest prayer for them and the attempt to be in our own lives such good advertisements for Christianity as will make it attractive.[19]

Here is one area of Lewis's beliefs where, though I hope he is right, I fear that he is mistaken. The recommended reading on this chapter will help you explore the issue further. As Lewis wrote, our time may be better spent not in speculation but in prayer, living as good examples and showing the attractiveness of Christ to people who need him.

So in response to the charge that Christianity is too narrow-minded, C. S. Lewis might say:

- You can be a committed Christian and not exclude the truth found in other religions.

- That which makes Christianity unique is also a cause of its exclusiveness: its historic claim to incarnation, God come in the flesh. Incarnation is either true or false.

- The claims of Christ either (1) show him to be an outrageous liar, (2) certify him as a lunatic, or (3) point to him as Lord. Faith in Christ is either of infinite importance or of no importance.

- Although Lewis believed that salvation is only through Christ, and that not everyone is saved, he did speculate that some who do not know the name of Jesus may be saved.

What is most important is not to perfectly understand all these issues but to believe in Jesus and to live as good representatives of his name.

THE ULTIMATE RELIGIOUS QUESTION

During the discussion John noticed that Julia brightened up at the mention of the "numinous." Now she says, "I've had many experiences of the numinous! Some people call it the holy, some call it the beyond . . ."

Lenae asks, "Weren't you scared?"

"No. Well, yes. In a way both—like Lewis said."

Simon is of course skeptical of any hint of the supernatural. "Those ex-

periences can be explained by electrical impulses on receptors in the brain. Or sometimes they're childhood memories that suddenly come to the surface. They could even be induced by a high fever. Once I had the flu and I kept seeing these hazy things floating around. It was weird, but it wasn't supernatural."

Mike says, "I think when Christians sing 'Holy, Holy, Holy,' they're not singing about influenza."

Brenda says, "I can't believe that all the religions got started just because somebody had hallucinations. Some religions, maybe. The crazy ones. But what's crazy to one person may not be crazy to another. It's confusing."

Lenae sits forward in her chair and says, "I think Hindus would be offended by what Lewis said about Hinduism. Good thing we don't have any Hindus in this group." She looks around doubtfully. "Do we?"

John says, "Even if we do, it wouldn't bother Lewis. He would welcome a good discussion with someone of any religion. And no matter what else they talked about, he would want to discuss what their respective faiths say about the ultimate question: what is our eternal destiny?"

"You mean what happens when we die?" Damon asks. "That's one I've thought about a lot. And I have to say I haven't found an answer I can live with." Damon's voice becomes casual, but he can't hide a shadow of strain. "So . . . what did our friend Mr. Lewis think about life after death?"

DEATH AND IMMORTALITY

Is Death Really the End of It All?

A̲s John is about to answer Damon's question, Julia jumps in and says, "I believe the soul never dies. We are reborn in an endless cycle of reincarnations. The wheel of life continues."

"You already know what I believe," says Simon. "When you die, you're dead. That's all there is to it. You have to do as much living as you can in this life, because this is the only chance you get."

Damon responds, "I tend to agree with you, but on the other hand I hope you're wrong."

"I believe in heaven," Lenae says, although not very firmly. "I think heaven is whatever you make it. It could be different for each person. And I think hell is here on earth. In war and poverty and hatred."

"I saw the movie about C. S. Lewis—Shadowlands," Mike offers. "In that movie it said that Lewis's future wife Joy was drawn to him partly because of his ideas about heaven."

Brenda speaks up. "I'll bet I know what Lewis's idea of heaven was! He *was such a book lover, I'll bet he thought heaven was one gigantic library. Or bookstore like this one. Well, maybe not like this one. Someplace where all the books in the universe could be found free." She frowns a little. "But somehow I think it must have been more than that." She looks at John. "What was his idea of heaven?"*

COMING TO TERMS WITH DEATH

For C. S. Lewis death was not a subject for abstract theories. While he was still young he had a number of painful encounters with death. His mother died when he was only nine. As a young man he lost friends in war, particularly his friend Paddy Moore. Later he lost his father, and finally—most painful of all—he lost his beloved wife Joy.

Lewis knew well that every worldview must come to terms with the question, Are we mere mortals or are we immortals? If a religion or philosophy dodges the question of death, it is inadequate for life in the real world.

Physical death is unavoidable. But is death the end? Different worldviews answer the question of life after death in radically different and contradictory ways. We can first consider the widest divergence, that of atheism and Christianity. This chart sums up their differences:

	Origin	Humankind	Destiny
Atheist	death	life	death
Christian	life	life	life

According to the atheist, life came spontaneously out of the cosmic slime. All life arose from inert or nonliving matter. Life came from nonlife through evolution. In other words, our origin is out of death. Since there is no life after death, our destiny is death. *Life is merely an unnecessary, temporary interruption in the midst of cosmic death.* No wonder atheist Bertrand Russell said that his view led to "unyielding despair." No wonder atheist Albert Camus maintained that the only really serious philosophical question is whether to commit suicide.

By contrast, for the Christian believer, our origin is out of life and our destiny is life. The living God is our Creator. Life is the gift God gives us. Our destiny in Christ is eternal life with him. Death is a serious and horrific thing; however, death is merely a temporary interruption in the midst of cosmic life.

Among worldviews, atheism is an aberration. Most societies throughout history have believed that death is not the end. But if that is true, what happens next? Are we reborn in a series of reincarnations? Are we rewarded? Punished? Do we continue as individual persons? Are we dissolved into a great All?

In Hinduism, our destiny (Shankara) is to transcend this world of illusory distinctions. Our goal is to be merged with the One, as a drop of water is absorbed into the ocean. The destiny of Buddhism (Theravada) is to extinguish desire, as one might blow out the flame of a candle. In Sanskrit, the word *Nirvana* comes from a root word meaning to be extinguished—to be blown out. Since there is no self, then there is no self to exist after death.

By contrast, believers in Christ maintain that the human predicament is our broken relationship with God, and the solution is reconciliation with God through Jesus Christ. We will enjoy this restored relationship for all eternity.

There is not much practical difference between the Hindu and Buddhist views of our destiny. Absorption and extinction amount to the same thing, in the sense that both lead to the loss of personality and individuality. By contrast, Christians look forward to the eternal extension of our individuality and our personal relationship of love with God and our fellow human beings.

No Mere Mortals

Since the question of life after death is so central to human experience, it is not surprising that C. S. Lewis often meditated on immortality. In fact, Lewis scholar Walter Hooper argues that C. S. Lewis's central theme was that all men and women are immortals. Lewis wrote:

> It is a serious thing to live in a society of possible gods and goddesses and to remember that the dullest and most uninteresting person you may talk to may one day be a creature which, if you saw it now, you would be strongly tempted to worship or else a horror and corruption such as you now meet if at all only in a nightmare. All day long we are in some degree helping each other to one or the other of these destinations. It is in light of these overwhelming possibilities, it is with the awe and the circumspection proper to them, that we should conduct all our dealings with one another, all friendships, all loves, all play, all politics. There are no ordinary people. You have never met a mere mortal. Nations, cultures, arts, civilizations, these are mortal and their life is to ours as the life of a gnat. But it is immortals that we joke with, work with, marry, snub, and exploit—immortal horrors or everlasting splendors.[1]

His belief in the immortality of every person was not an abstraction for Lewis. He lived his belief in his everyday life. His tireless correspondence is perhaps evidence that he truly believed "there are no ordinary people." Lewis responded personally to every person who wrote him. At the height of his popularity Lewis's correspondence consumed hours of every day. At a conference of the C. S. Lewis Institute a woman brought a copy of a beautifully handwritten letter Lewis had written her when she was six years old. She had read *The Lion, the Witch and the Wardrobe* and wrote to Lewis to tell him how Aslan had pointed her toward Christ. Much of Lewis's remarkable correspondence is now collected in *The Letters of C. S. Lewis, Letters to an American Lady, Letters to Children, Letters to Calabria* and so on. Many more of his letters are in private hands and have never been published.

Even when he became a popular author, Lewis did not elevate his standard of living. He gave away most if not all of the proceeds from his books. He continued to live in the same modest house, he stayed with the same rather shabby professional wardrobe, and he never bought a car because he never learned to drive. He did not travel widely. He never came to the United States, and in fact he seldom crossed the English Channel. He put his money into an "agape fund" and gave it away—so much, in fact, that a friend had to advise him to keep a third for taxes. Why did he give away so much (often anonymously) except that he believed he had "never met a mere mortal"?

Sometimes a person's deepest beliefs emerge in casual conversation. Once Walter Hooper and Lewis were talking about "a bore whom we both knew, a man who was generally recognized as being almost unbelievably dull. I told Lewis that the man succeeded in interesting me by the very intensity of his boredom. Yes, he said, but let us not forget that our Lord might well have said, 'As ye have done it unto one of the least of these my bores, you have done it unto me.' "[2]

Such a view of life gives tremendous significance not only to individual people but to individual choices. Lewis says that in every choice, we pick the beatific or the miserific vision. In *Mere Christianity* he writes:

> Every time you make a choice, you are turning the central part
> of you, the part that chooses, into something a little different

from what it was before. . . . You are slowly turning this central thing either into a heavenly creature or a hellish creature. . . . To be one kind of creature is heaven: that is joy and peace and knowledge and power. To be the other means madness, horror, idiocy, rage, impotence, and eternal loneliness. Each of us at each moment is progressing to one state or the other.[3]

THE PARADOX OF REWARDS

When Lewis first came to faith, he really did not think about eternal life but focused on enjoying God in this life. He paralleled his experience with Old Testament people who did not have a clear understanding of heaven. They recognized that "He [God] and nothing else is their goal and the satisfaction of their needs, and that He has a claim on them simply by being what He is, quite apart from anything He can bestow or deny."[4] Lewis later said that the years he spent without the focus on heavenly rewards "always seem to me to have been of great value" because they taught him to delight in God above any prospect of reward.

Lewis never disparaged the place of heavenly rewards; later he delighted in them. But he saw that the paradox of reward might be a stumbling block for some. On the one hand, the purest faith in God believes in him for nothing and is disinterested in any benefits to follow. On the other hand, if a reward is received for what is done, the prospect might pander to self-interest and greed. Lewis discusses this paradox in *English Literature in the Sixteenth Century:*

Tyndale, as regards to the natural condition of humanity, holds by nature we can do no good works without respect of some profit either in this world or in the world to come. . . . That the profit should be located in another world means, as Tyndale clearly sees, no difference! Theological hedonism is still hedonism. Whether the man is seeking heaven or a hundred pounds, he can still but seek himself, of freedom in the true sense—of spontaneity or disinterestedness—nature knows nothing. And yet by a terrible paradox such disinterestedness is precisely what the moral law demands.[5]

One way to resolve the tension between disinterestedness and rewards is to realize that self-interest is not the same thing as selfishness. Jesus appeals to self-interest as a motive for self-denial. I have been told that Mark 8:35-36 is Lewis's most quoted passage of Scripture. Here Jesus says, "For whoever wants to save his life will lose it, but whoever loses his life for me and for the gospel will save it. What good is it for a man to gain the whole world, yet forfeit his soul?"

Unless we have sufficient reason to sacrifice something we love, the cost will always be too great. Jesus gives us sufficient reason to pay the cost. First, if we try to save our lives by seeking our own pleasure in our own way, we will lose not only eternal life but the fullness of life right now. Second, if we "lose our lives"—give them away to Christ and others—we will gain not only eternal life but the fullness of life in the present.

Jesus' argument here is that self-denial is in our self-interest. If we say no to ourselves and follow him, we will gain everything worth having. Self-interest does not necessarily make our motives impure. Lewis says in *The Problem of Pain*:

> We are afraid that heaven is a bribe and that if we make it our goal we shall no longer be disinterested. It is not so. Heaven offers nothing a mercenary soul can desire. It is safe to tell the pure in heart that they shall see God, for only the pure in heart want to. There are rewards that do not sully motives. A man's

love for a woman is not mercenary because he wants to marry her, nor his love for poetry mercenary because he wants to read it, nor his love for exercise less disinterested because he wants to run and leap and walk. Love by its very nature seeks to enjoy its object.[6]

When we are lost in the wonder, awe and praise of God, we are the happiest we can become, but also the least self-conscious. When we are focused on God, we are not focused on self. The same dynamic shows up in a close friendship. With people we do not know well, we may feel self-conscious and worry about how they perceive us. But with a good friend we can lose ourselves in conversation, conveying deep feelings with no self-centeredness. Lewis summarizes this unself-conscious experience: "The happiest moments are when we forget our precious selves . . . but have everything else (God, our fellow humans, the animals, the garden and the sky) instead."[7] In this experience we are doing that which is in the interest of our own joy but not selfishly. We are joyous but disinterested.

IMAGES OF HEAVEN

The movie *Shadowlands* claims that Joy Gresham fell in love with C. S. Lewis because of his images of heaven. Although there was more to it than that, Lewis's images of heaven are glorious.

My professor John Gerstner, who always conducted his classes by dialecture (dialogue), once asked us, "Who has ever been perfect?" We came up with Jesus and with Adam and Eve before the Fall, but then we ran out of examples. When we gave up, Dr. Gerstner said, "You've just missed countless millions of people." We asked, "Who do you mean?" He responded, "All those who have died and are now in heaven with Christ."

C. S. Lewis shares something of the same insight toward the end
of *The Silver Chair.* At this point the children were in Aslan's country
beyond Narnia. King Caspian lay dead under a clear stream. They all
wept, even Aslan. Aslan told Eustace to get a thorn and push it into
his lion paw. As a result, a drop of blood fell into the stream and King
Caspian leaped up alive, no longer old, but a young man. He rushed
to Aslan

> and flung his arms as far as he could go around the lion's neck
> and he gave him the strong kisses of a king, and Aslan gave him
> the wild kisses of a lion.
>
> Eustace was afraid to touch the dead. "Look here! I say," he
> stammered, "It's all very well. But aren't you—? I mean, Didn't
> you—?"
>
> "Oh, don't be such an ass," said Caspian. "But," said Eustace,
> looking at Aslan, "hasn't he—er—died?"
>
> "Yes," said the Lion. "He has died. Most people have, you
> know? Even I have. There are very few that haven't."[8]

In other words, if our eyes could be opened for just a moment to
the eternal dimension in the present, it would change our view of
both death and life. Many more people have died and now live than
those who are presently on earth.

My favorite passage in what has become my favorite of the Narnia chronicles is at the conclusion of *The Last Battle.* In the chapter
"Farewell to Shadowlands" the children are afraid of being sent
back to England. Aslan assures them that this time they will not
have to go. A "wild hope" arises in them. Aslan tells them that their
transition to Narnia from a train (in the beginning of the book) was
because there was a real railway accident. In the final paragraph
Aslan tells them:

"Your father and mother and all of you are—as you used to call it in the Shadowlands—dead. The term is over: the holiday has begun. The dream is ended. This is the morning." . . . The things that began to happen after that were so great and beautiful that I cannot write them. And as for us, this is the end of all the stories, and we can most truly say that they all lived happily ever after. But for them, it was only the beginning of the real story. All their life in this world and all their adventures in Narnia have only been the cover and title page; now at last they were beginning chapter one of the Great Story which none on earth has read; which goes on forever, in which every chapter is better than the one before.[9]

LEWIS'S OWN DEATH

Why do people die when they do? We will get no clear answer in this life. But perhaps if we saw it all from their point of view or from an eternal perspective, everything would look differently. Lewis writes: "Heaven will solve our problems, but not by showing us subtle reconciliations between all our apparently contradictory notions. The notions will be knocked from under our feet. We will see that there never was any problem."[10]

Lewis faced his own death bravely and calmly. When he had to decline a certain lecture invitation that he would have enjoyed, his face grew sad; then he said simply, "Send them a polite refusal."[11] Once, close to the end, he passed into a coma from which he was not expected to emerge. When he awoke, Lewis was rather disappointed to realize that, like Lazarus (raised by Jesus after four days in the tomb), he had his dying to do all over again.

HOW CAN WE KNOW?

How can we know that these things are true? Are they only childish hopes? It comes down to the credibility of Jesus Christ and to the reality of Christ's resurrection from the dead. If Christ was raised from the dead, then he provides the guarantee that we will be raised. If Christ was not raised, then as the apostle Paul said, our faith is futile, we are still in our sins, and we might as well eat, drink and be merry for tomorrow we die (see 1 Corinthians 15). If Christ was lying when he told us about eternal life, we should utterly reject him as demonic for telling us such a cruel untruth. If he told the truth about eternal life, then he is our risen Lord.

Not only is there a strong historical case for the resurrection of Christ,[12] but millions of people have testified and continue to testify that his living presence has changed them in radical ways. Could whopping lies or raving lunacy transform people's lives from insanity to sanity, from slavery to freedom, from hostility to love, from instability to stability, from brokenness to wholeness?

Skeptics ridicule Christian believers whose hopes are set on heaven. We are accused of being so heavenly minded that we are no earthly good. Lewis argues that it is the other way around. Those who are the most heavenly minded have been and are the most earthly good. He says, "If you read history, you will find that the Christians who did most for the present world were just those who thought most of the next. . . . It is since Christians have largely ceased to think of the other world that they have become so ineffective in this. Aim at Heaven and you will get earth 'thrown in'; aim at earth and you will get neither."[13]

ALL IMMORTAL

John takes a deep breath, looks around the circle and says, "I'll say what I think C. S. Lewis would say if he were here. It makes all the difference whether we see each other as just physical bodies that are here by accident or immortal beings created by God, who are going to live forever. And when I look at you, I see six immortals."

Mike says, "Seven. Don't leave yourself out."

Quickly Julia says, "I agree with the immortality of the soul. Our souls have always existed and will always exist. We have all taken on and will continue to take on a series of physical bodies." John thinks he detects a slight change in Julia's voice, as though her remark is more a recitation than a statement of conviction.

Damon says, "I think Lewis means something more than just that our souls don't die. He means we're all going somewhere."

"And it sounds like it's one of two destinations. Kind of an old-fashioned idea," Brenda points out.

John smiles and replies, "Well, we've seen all along that Lewis stood squarely in the stream of classic Christian belief. He didn't offer any great innovations. He presented Christ—sometimes in fiction, sometimes straight out—and he said, 'Okay, what will you decide about him?' "

Lenae asks, "Why do we have to decide anything about Christ? He just is. We can't decide anything about that."

John acknowledges, "You're right, we can't decide anything that would change Christ. But what we decide about him will change us."

At last Simon speaks up. "If we decide to follow Christ's teachings, of course it'll change us. Jesus was a great moral teacher. After he died, the stories about him got inflated, until his followers got this idea that he was a miracle worker and the Son of God."

"But what if they were right and he was those things?" Brenda asks. "Lewis said it matters"—she looks at John—"doesn't it?"

CHRIST

Isn't Jesus Just Another Good, Moral Teacher?

"Yes, Lewis said that what we think of Christ definitely matters," says John in reply to Brenda's question. "In fact I'd say that Jesus stands at the very center of C. S. Lewis's writings. In his apologetic works—where he makes a case for Christianity—obviously Christ is central. In his fiction, Jesus is very close in the background if not explicitly at the center of Lewis's mind."

"That's Aslan the lion, right?" Damon asks.

"Yes, but it's interesting to discover, a lion as Jesus wasn't Lewis's original intent. Before he wrote **The Lion, the Witch and the Wardrobe**, he had been having dreams about lions. Also an image came to his mind of a faun and a lamppost. That's how it all started."

"Weird," says Lenae.

"Imaginative," says Brenda.

John says, "Lewis made it clear that he didn't want the Chronicles of Narnia to be seen as a precise allegory with a one-to-one relationship be-

tween everything in Narnia and his own beliefs. But obviously there are parallels. We could say that as Aslan is to Narnia, so Jesus is to our world."

Simon repeats, "He's a great moral teacher," and John responds, "OK, let's find out."

NOT SAFE BUT GOOD

In *The Lion, the Witch and the Wardrobe*, soon after the children arrive in Narnia for the first time, their new friend Mr. Beaver tells them: "They say Aslan is on the move—perhaps has already landed." When the children first hear the name Aslan it stirs each of them in a different way:

"Edmund felt a sensation of mysterious horror. Peter felt suddenly brave and adventurous. Susan felt as if some delicious smell or some delicious strain of music had just floated by her. And Lucy got the feeling you have when you wake up in the morning and realize that it is the beginning of summer."[1]

They find out that Aslan is a king and hear about an old rhyme, a kind of prophecy:

Wrong will be right, when Aslan comes in sight,
At the sound of his roar, sorrows will be no more,
When he bares his teeth, winter meets its death,
And when he shakes his mane, we will have spring again.[2]

Susan asks, "Is he quite safe?" "Safe?" said Mr. Beaver, " . . . 'Course he isn't safe. But he's good."[3]

Eventually Aslan appears and the battle between good and evil begins in earnest. As the story unfolds, Aslan shows up when and where he will. He does not appear often, almost never on demand, and always at his own discretion. And he does not have to be visible in order for his power to be felt.

Throughout Lewis's Narnia stories we see in Aslan the attributes of Jesus. He is always present, whether or not we are aware of him. He is always working for our good, whether or not we understand (or even like) what he does. He transforms us in ways we could never do for ourselves. Greatest of all, he has sacrificed his life for us and has risen again to free us from the bondage of sin.

The lion who is always with us. In *The Horse and His Boy,* a young boy named Shasta has grown up not knowing his real mother and father. A fisherman has brought him up but has been very harsh to him. Once when a soldier passes through, Shasta overhears them bargaining over the price for which he will be sold into slavery. He escapes with a talking horse. They have many adventures—they are chased by lions, have to swim for their lives, spend a night among tombs with wild beasts howling all around, and are chased by another lion that wounds their companion Aravis.

Toward the end of the book Shasta is walking in the dark when he becomes aware that something is walking beside him. His imagination runs wild. Perhaps it is a giant (he had heard of such in this country) or even worse, a ghost. When Shasta speaks, a large voice answers and assures him that it is neither a giant nor a ghost. The voice asks Shasta to tell him his sorrowful story. When Shasta completes his story—especially the parts about lions—they have the following conversation:

> "I do not call you unfortunate," said the Large Voice.
>
> "Don't you think it was bad luck to meet so many lions?" said Shasta.
>
> "There was only one lion," said the Voice.
>
> "What on earth do you mean? I've told you there were at least two the first night, and—"

"There was only one: but he was swift of foot."

"How do you know?"

"I was the lion." And as Shasta gaped with open mouth and said nothing, the Voice continued. "I was the lion who forced you to join Aravis. I was the cat who comforted you among the houses of the dead. I was the lion who drove the jackals from you while you slept. I was the lion who gave the Horses new strength of fear for the last mile so that you should reach King Lune in time. And I was the lion you do not remember who pushed the boat in which you lay, a child near death, so that it came to shore where a man sat, wakeful at night, to receive you."

"Then it was you who wounded Aravis?"

"It was I."

"But what for?"

"Child," said the Voice, "I am telling you your story, not hers. I tell no-one any story but his own."[4]

Like Christ, Aslan is ever present and works in his own mysterious ways for our good, even though at the moment his ways may not be pleasant.

The lion who transforms us. In *The Voyage of the Dawn Treader* Eustace (the most spoiled of the lot) is turned into a dragon. He is feeling sorry for himself and quite uncomfortable with his predicament when a Lion approaches him in the moonlight and communicates to Eustace that he must follow. The Lion leads him into the mountains to a well within a garden. The Lion then indicates that Eustace needs to undress in order to bathe. But of course Eustace, now a dragon, is not wearing any clothes. Eustace thinks the Lion means he should shed his outer layer of skin, as a snake does. He scratches himself and a scaly outer layer does come off. Eustace hurries to bathe in the well—only to see in the reflection that he is still a dragon. He tries it again and again but is still a dragon. Finally Eustace realizes that he must let the Lion undress him. By now he is desperate enough to let the Lion do this. Later Eustace tells the other children:

> "The first tear he made was so deep that I thought it had gone right into my heart. And when he began pulling the skin off, it hurt worse than anything I have ever felt. The only thing that made me able to bear it was just the pleasure of feeling the stuff peel off. You know—if you've ever picked the scab of a sore place. It hurts like billy-oh but it is fun to see it coming away."[5]

Eustace was "undragoned" in more ways than one. He was transformed from the inside out. Afterward he was a different boy. Like Eustace, we need the Lion (Christ) to transform us from the inside out, and we are powerless to do it ourselves.

The lion who sacrifices himself. In *The Lion, the Witch and the Wardrobe* there is a confrontation between the White Witch and Aslan. She comes to claim the life of Edmund because he has turned traitor. She appeals to a deep magic from the beginning of time, saying that "every traitor belongs to me as my lawful prey and that for every treachery I have a right to a kill."[6]

Aslan and the Witch talk privately, and Aslan declares Edmund free from the Witch's claim. But the look of joy on the Witch's face as she departs and her allusion to a promise Aslan has made indicate that something ominous is about to happen. Late that night Aslan leaves the camp "head hung low" and walking slowly.[7] As Lucy and Susan watch from a distance in horror and disbelief, the Witch and all manner of evil creatures bind Aslan to the Stone Table, shave him and muzzle him. Finally the Witch takes a stone knife and kills Aslan.

Exhausted by grief, Lucy and Susan wait for morning. As the sun rises, they hear a loud crack and see that the Stone Table has broken in two. But there is no Aslan.

"Who's done it?" cried Susan. "What does it mean? Is it more magic?"

"Yes!" said a great voice behind their backs. "It's more magic."[8]

Aslan is alive! He is real, not a ghost. He licks Susan's forehead. The girls are overjoyed and throw themselves on him, kissing him repeatedly. When they calm down, Susan asks:

"But what does it all mean?" . . .

"It means," said Aslan, "that though the Witch knew the Deep Magic, there is a magic deeper still which she did not know. Her knowledge goes back only to the dawn of Time. But if she could have looked a little further back, into the stillness and the darkness before Time dawned, she would have read there a different incantation. She would have known that when a willing victim who had committed no treachery was killed in a traitor's stead, the Table would crack and Death itself would start working backwards."[9]

Just as Aslan was killed in Edmund's stead and saved his life, so Jesus' death for us not only takes away our guilt for what we have done or left undone; it begins to transform us from the inside out, from death to new life that will go on through eternity.

LIAR, LUNATIC OR LORD?

Perhaps the best known and most crucial passage C. S. Lewis wrote about Jesus Christ appears in *Mere Christianity,* where Lewis argues that Christ cannot be simply a great moral teacher and nothing else.

> I am trying here to prevent anyone saying the really foolish thing that people often say about Him: "I am ready to accept Jesus as a great moral teacher, but I don't accept His claim to be God." That is the one thing we must not say. A man who was really a man and said the sort of things Jesus said would not be a great moral teacher. He would either be a lunatic—on the level with the man who says he is a poached egg—or else he would be the Devil of Hell. You must make your choice. Either this man was, and is, the Son of God, or else a madman or something worse. You can shut Him up for a fool, you can spit at Him and kill Him as a demon, or you can fall at His feet and call Him Lord and God. But let us not come with any patronizing nonsense about His being a great human teacher. He has not left that open to us. He did not intend to.[10]

But did Jesus actually claim to be more than a teacher? It is clear that he did, both directly and indirectly. When he said, "Before Abraham was born, I am" (John 8:58), he identified himself with the name of God in the Old Testament. When he said, "No one knows the Son except the Father, and no one knows the Father except the Son and those to whom the Son chooses to reveal him" (Matthew 11:27), he asserted a peer relationship with God the Father. Jesus repeatedly set forth belief in himself as a condition of salvation. He also claimed to be the good shepherd (John 10:11), the bread of life (John 6:35), the resurrection and the life (John 11:25), the true vine (John 15:1) and the light of the world (John 8:12). He even claimed that he could forgive sins, knowing very well his enemies' opinion that only God can forgive sins (Mark 2:10).

If a mere human being made such claims, knowing they were untrue, he would be the world's biggest charlatan. If he made such claims and believed them, he would be history's greatest case of egomania or insanity.

CLAIMS THAT CAUSED CONTROVERSY

But did Jesus' contemporaries understand the radical nature of his claims? Undoubtedly they did. He caused a major controversy when he healed a blind man and claimed to be the light of the world, and then shortly afterward called himself the good shepherd. People got into a furious debate about who he was. "Many of them said, 'He is demon-possessed and raving mad. Why listen to him?'

"But others said, 'These are not the sayings of a man possessed by a demon. Can a demon open the eyes of the blind?' " (John 10:20-21).

The religious Jews who heard Jesus knew their own Scriptures thoroughly. They recognized that Jesus was claiming equality with God, and their reactions show they were incensed by his words. When he used the name of God "I AM" for himself and said he existed before Abraham, his hearers "picked up stones to stone him" (John 8:58-59). They did the same thing when he said, "I and the Father are one" (John 10:30-31). When he said, "the Father is in me, and I in the Father," they "tried to seize him"—that is, to arrest him (John 10:38-39). What they did not say was "He makes some outlandish claims, but he is a wonderful moral teacher."

EITHER-OR

We wind up faced with two options. What Jesus Christ said about himself is either true or false. We can trace the logical conclusions of both options:

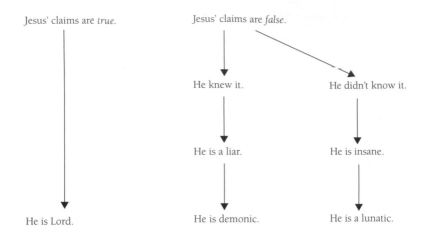

Jesus' claims are *true.*   Jesus' claims are *false.*

He knew it.   He didn't know it.

He is a liar.   He is insane.

He is Lord.   He is demonic.   He is a lunatic.

Some would offer another option: that the character of Jesus is a myth or a legend, and if he lived at all, he did not make the statements attributed to him in Scripture. We have dealt with that objection in chapter five on myth.

WHAT DO YOU DECIDE?

C. S. Lewis did a masterful job of condensing the question of Jesus to its essence: Is Jesus a liar, a lunatic or Lord? It is left to each of us to answer.

Is he a liar? It would be very strange if the teachings of a liar would encourage people to walk in the way of scrupulous honesty. Throughout church history, committed Christians have been known as people who keep their word even at great cost to themselves.

Is he a lunatic? Then it is impossible to explain the amazing rationality of his teachings about relationships, or the perfect balance of justice and mercy in his life. And how do we account for the effect of his "lunacy" on his followers? The weak become strong; the selfish, selfless; the defeated, victorious; the bad, good.

Is he Lord? If Jesus is Lord, the fact is of more than intellectual interest. It demands a response. We can either deny his authority or we can submit to it.

We can confirm Jesus' claims through evidence, but ultimately we must test them through experience. Jesus said that if we choose to do God's will, then will we "find out whether my teaching comes from God or whether I speak on my own" (John 7:17). He also promised, "If you hold to my teaching, you are really my disciples. Then you will know the truth, and the truth will set you free" (John 8:32).

If Jesus is who he says he is, and if he is risen from the dead, then he is available for a relationship with us here and now. We can admire a beautiful cake and say it would be good to eat, but we can know its goodness only if we go ahead and taste it. We can discuss and study Jesus, but we will know that he is true only if we trust and commit ourselves to him.

The Beginning

One by one the members of the study group get up from their chairs. All seem reluctant to leave. Julia steps over to John, grips his hand and says, "Thank you. It's been fascinating. I feel as though I've dipped my toe into some new waters."

"Well Julia, to continue your metaphor, don't be afraid to take the plunge," John says. Julia gives his hand a final squeeze and walks away.

John approaches Simon with hand outstretched, and Simon gives him a surprisingly firm handshake. John says, "I have a confession to make. I hope you'll forgive me. It took me a while to stop thinking of you as 'the atheist of our group.'" Simon laughs and says, "I'm used to that. To be honest, I started out thinking of you as the right-wing religious fanatic of the group."

Lenae is sorting through the stack of C. S. Lewis books on the table. "I gotta read more of this," she says. "If I just had more time."

As John is about to say that we find time for what's important to us, Brenda walks up to him, looks directly into his eyes and shakes his hand so vigorously that the bangles on her bracelet clank together. She says only, "Thank you. Thank you." Then she leaves.

John is left wondering. He hears Damon's voice behind him. "Thanks, John. This wasn't always the most pleasant group to be in, but . . ."

"Really? Why? What could I have done to make it better?"

"It wasn't you. It's just that I had to think about things I didn't want to think about. C. S. Lewis makes you do that, doesn't he?"

As Damon leaves, Lenae turns from the pile of books and remarks, "Sometimes this group gave me a headache. Too much thinking. But it's all really new to me. Thanks, John; it's given me something to think about." She looks at her watch. "Oh, I have to get moving," she says and hurries out.

Slowly John picks up his books and turns to leave. He sees Mike and says, "Thanks for coming. I wish you'd said a little more."

"Guess I only talk when I've got something to say," Mike answers. Then he turns toward Simon, who John is surprised to find still standing nearby. Mike puts a hand on Simon's shoulder and says, "Hey, how about if we go over to the café. You look like you could use another cup of coffee."

As they walk away, John has an impulse to say more, "Simon, would you be interested in continuing to consider spiritual questions?"

Simon turns, looks at the floor, hesitates, but finally responds, "You know, I would like to do that. I hate to admit it, but I am no longer as certain of my atheism as when we began this study."

He motions to John. "Why don't you join us for coffee?"

As John, Mike and Simon walk toward the café, Simon adds, "I think I'd like to read some of Lewis's books for myself. Where do you recommend I start?"

John replies, "I can give you a good reading list, but remember faith in Christ is more than just satisfying your intellect. C. S. Lewis would not want people to focus on his personality or even his books. He wanted to point beyond that to Jesus."

Recommended Reading

Chapter 1: Why Consider C. S. Lewis's Arguments for Christ?

Como, James T., ed. *C. S. Lewis at the Breakfast Table and Other Reminiscences.* New York: Harcourt Brace, 1992. Many stories of encounters with Lewis from his friends and acquaintances can be enjoyed from this book.

Gresham, Douglas. *Lenten Lands.* London: Collins, 1989. This is a valuable personal account by C. S. Lewis's stepson.

Sayer, George. *Jack: C. S. Lewis and His Times.* New York: Harper & Row, 1988. This is the best overall biography of C. S. Lewis.

Chapter 2: What Were Lewis's Obstacles to Faith?

Lewis, C. S. *Surprised by Joy: The Shape of My Early Life.* New York: Harcourt Brace, 1984. C. S. Lewis's own account of his journey to faith in Christ.

Markos, Louis. *Lewis Agonistes: How C. S. Lewis Can Train Us to Wrestle With the Modern and Postmodern World.* Nashville: Broadman & Holman, 2003. As the title suggests, this book shows the issues Lewis wrestled with and applies his insights to the contemporary world.

Purtill, Richard. *C. S. Lewis' Case for the Christian Faith.* San Francisco: Harper & Row, 1981. A helpful work that examines some of Lewis's obstacles to faith and shows how he overcame them.

Chapter 3: Chronological Snobbery

Lewis, C. S. "De Descriptione Temporium." In *Selected Literary Essays.* Edited by Walter Hooper. Cambridge: Cambridge University Press, 1969. Lewis's classic address on why you need to listen to dinosaurs such as he.

————. "Is Progress Possible?" In *God in the Dock: Essays on Theology and Ethics*. Edited by Walter Hooper. Grand Rapids: Eerdmans, 1970. Lewis questions the promise of "progress" in the political realm.

————. "On the Reading of Old Books." In *God in the Dock: Essays on Theology and Ethics*. Edited by Walter Hooper. Grand Rapids: Eerdmans, 1970. Lewis's classic essay on the need for ancient perspective in the modern world.

————. "On the Transmission of Christianity." In *First and Second Things: Essays on Theology and Ethics*. Edited by Walter Hooper. Glasgow: Collins, 1985. Lewis on how faith can be passed from one generation to the next.

Chapter 4: The Problem of Evil

Geisler, Norman. *The Roots of Evil*. Grand Rapids: Zondervan, 1978. A very good discussion on how everyone has a problem of evil as well as how Christianity has addressed this issue.

Lewis, C. S. *A Grief Observed*. New York: Bantam Books, 1976.

————. *The Problem of Pain*. New York: Macmillan, 1969.

Nash, Ronald. *Faith and Reason*. Grand Rapids: Zondervan, 1988. See pp. 177-221 in particular. An excellent study of the problem of evil dealing with the deductive and inductive problem as well as "gratuitous" evil.

Plantinga, Alvin. *God, Freedom, and Evil*. Grand Rapids: Eerdmans, 1974. A classic philosophical study on this issue.

Chapter 5: Myth

Garlow, James, and Peter Jones. *Cracking DaVinci's Code*. Colorado Springs: Victor, 2004. Perhaps the most readable of the responses to *The DaVinci Code*. This phenomenon has arisen because Brown's book brings together the latest critiques of Christianity.

Lewis, C. S. "Christian Apologetics." In *God in the Dock: Essays on Theology and Ethics*. Grand Rapids: Eerdmans, 1970. Lewis's classic essays including a short discussion of the "Thick" and "Clear" religions.

"The Mythology of Joseph Campbell." *Spiritual Counterfeits Project Journal*, 9, no. 2 (1990). Contact SCP at P. O. Box, 4308 Berkeley, California 94704, telephone 510-540-0300. Valuable resource on evaluating Joseph Campbell.

Wilkins, Michael, and J. P. Moreland, eds. *Jesus Under Fire: Modern Scholarship Reinvents the Historical Jesus.* Grand Rapids: Zondervan, 1995. This book critiques the Jesus Seminar type of approach to the Bible.

Wright, N. T. *The Challenge of Jesus: Rediscovering Who Jesus Was and Is.* Downers Grove, Ill.: InterVarsity Press, 1999. An outstanding study of the issues involved in the historical Jesus debate. It summarizes what he more fully discusses in his larger works.

Chapter 6: Rationalism

Lewis, C. S. *The Pilgrim's Regress: An Allegorical Apology for Christianity, Reason, and Romanticism.* Grand Rapids: Eerdmans, 1989. Lewis's early response to the views held in his time.

Chapter 7: Imagination

Carnell, Corbin Scott. *Bright Shadow of Reality: C. S. Lewis and the Feeling Intellect.* Grand Rapids: Eerdmans, 1974. A very helpful work showing the place of imagination and desire as a significant part of C. S. Lewis's perspective.

Downing, David. *Planets in Peril: A Critical Study of C. S. Lewis's Ransom Trilogy.* Amherst: University of Massachusetts Press, 1992. An excellent study of Lewis's space trilogy.

Lindskoog, Kathryn Ann. *C. S. Lewis: Mere Christian.* Glendale, Calif.: G/L Publications, 1973. A great introduction to the whole scope of Lewis's thought.

Chapter 8: Miracles

Geisler, Norman. *Miracles and the Modern Mind.* Grand Rapids: Baker, 1992. A helpful study by an excellent philosopher.

Geivett, R. Douglas, and Gary R. Habermas, eds. *In Defense of Miracles.* Downers Grove, Ill.: InterVarsity Press, 1997. An excellent set of essays by different authors on various aspects of miracles.

Lewis, C. S. *Miracles*. New York: Collier, 1947. C. S. Lewis's important study
clearing the way to evaluate the miraculous.

Nash, Ronald. *Faith and Reason: Searching for a Rational Faith*. Grand Rapids:
Zondervan, 1988. See especially pp. 225-72. An excellent response to
Hume's critique of miracles as well as a development of Lewis's critique
of naturalism.

Reppert, Victor. *C. S. Lewis's Dangerous Idea: A Philosophical Defense of Lewis's
Argument from Reason*. Downers Grove, Ill.: InterVarsity Press, 2003. This
book defends Lewis's argument against naturalism from philosophical
criticisms. Lewis and Reppert's argument is dangerous to atheists and biological determinists of our day.

Chapter 9: Wish Fulfillment

Küng, Hans. *Freud and the Problem of God*. New Haven, Conn.: Yale University Press, 1979. An outstanding study on Freud's view of religion that
shows why his views are disregarded by modern scholars even though
they are still used in contemporary culture.

Nicholi, Armand. *The Question of God: C. S. Lewis and Sigmund Freud Debate
God, Love, Sex and the Meaning of Life*. New York: Free Press, 2002. An excellent, readable study of Lewis's and Freud's views. This was made into
a PBS documentary. It is very much worth reading or watching.

Vitz, Paul C. *Sigmund Freud's Christian Unconscious*. New York: Guilford
Press, 1972. A fascinating study of the Christian influence on Freud's life
by a former atheist, Freudian, now a believer in Christ.

Chapter 10: Postmodernism

Carson, D. A. *The Gagging of God: Christianity Confronts Pluralism*. Grand
Rapids: Zondervan, 1996. A thorough examination of postmodernism,
pluralism and inclusivism.

Erickson, Millard. *Truth or Consequences*. Downers Grove, Ill.: InterVarsity
Press, 2001. The best book yet in providing a readable and thorough sur-
vey of postmodernism and how to address it.

Groothuis, Douglas. *Truth Decay*. Downers Grove, Ill.: InterVarsity Press,
2000. A guide to understanding the different views of truth people hold

and how to give a biblical response to them.

McCallum, Dennis, ed. *The Death of Truth.* Minneapolis: Bethany House, 1996. A helpful collection of essays on the impact of postmodernism on various arenas of life, such as healthcare, education, literature, history, law and science.

Chapter 11: Relativism

Adler, Mortimer. *Truth in Religion: The Plurality of Religions and the Unity of Truth.* New York: Collier, 1990. An account of Adler's move from paganism to theism, rejecting relativism and pantheism along the way. He later became a Christian.

Beckwith, Francis J., and Gregory Koukl. *Relativism: Feet Firmly Planted in Mid-Air.* Grand Rapids: Baker, 1998. A short critique of relativism and analysis of how it has influenced American society.

Kreeft, Peter. *A Refutation of Moral Relativism: Interview with an Absolutist.* San Francisco: Ignatius Press, 1999. An imaginary dialogue with many helpful insights and quotes.

Lewis, C. S. *Abolition of Man.* Oxford: Collier, 1947. C. S. Lewis's classic critique of relativism.

Lindsley, Art. *True Truth: Defending Absolute Truth in a Relativistic Age.* Downers Grove, Ill: InterVarsity Press, 2004. A look at how to maintain absolutes without absolutism. The first half of the book argues that faith in Christ is necessarily opposed to and inconsistent with an intolerant, self-righteous, arrogant, know-it-all, black and white, defensive mentality. It has an antidote that relativism lacks to these vices. The second half of the book develops an argument against relativism.

Chapter 12: Other Religions

Carson, D. A. *The Gagging of God: Christianity Confronts Pluralism.* Grand Rapids: Zondervan, 1996. An excellent, thorough discussion of pluralism and inclusivism.

Clark, David K., and Norman L. Geisler. *Apologetics in the New Age: A Christian Critique of Pantheism.* Grand Rapids: Baker, 1990. A great philosophical critique of pantheism.

Copleston, Fredrick. *Religion and the One: Philosophies East and West.* New York: Crossroad, 1982. An outstanding philosophical discussion of the all is One philosophy.

Davis, Philip G. *Goddess Unmasked: The Rise of Neopagan Feminist Spirituality.* Dallas: Spence, 1998. An outstanding recent book on neopaganism.

Hoyt, Karen, ed. *New Age Rage.* Old Tappan, N.J.: Revell, 1987. Helpful insights into various dimensions of the New Age Movement. My chapter is the last.

Mangalwadi, Vishal. *The World of Gurus.* New Delhi: Nivedit Good Books, 1987. A superb response to Hinduism from an articulate believer in India.

Nash, Ronald. *Is Jesus the Only Savior?* Grand Rapids: Zondervan, 1994. The best short summary of the debate.

Zacharias, Ravi. *Jesus Among Other Gods: The Absolute Claims of the Christian Message.* Nashville: Word, 2000. A winsome discussion of Christianity's relation to other religions by a great communicator.

———. *The Lotus and the Cross: Jesus Talks with Buddha.* Sisters, Ore.: Multnomah Publishers, 2001. A creative, imagined dialogue between Jesus and Buddha. Zacharias spent considerable time researching this book by talking with Buddhist monks. It is very helpful in getting to the roots, questions and problems with this significant influence on the New Age Movement in the West.

Chapter 13: Death and Immortality

Craig, William Lane. *The Son Rises: The Historical Evidence for the Resurrection of Jesus.* Chicago: Moody, 1981. Another concise argument for Christ's resurrection.

Kreeft, Peter, and Ronald K. Tacelli. *Handbook of Christian Apologetics: Hundreds of Answers to Crucial Questions.* Downers Grove, Ill.: InterVarsity Press, 1994. A wealth of arguments for Christianity as well as answers to criticisms. See especially chapter ten, "Life After Death."

Morison, Frank. *Who Moved the Stone?* Grand Rapids: Zondervan, 1977. Classic defense of the resurrection of Christ by a lawyer who set out to disprove it.

Chapter 14: Christ

Lewis, C. S. *Mere Christianity.* New York: Touchstone, 1996. Lewis's classic statement of Christianity. If you read nothing else of Lewis, read this book.

Strobel, Lee. *The Case for Christ.* Grand Rapids: Zondervan, 1998. Excellent, easy-to-read summary of evidences for Christ.

NOTES

Chapter One: Why Consider C. S. Lewis's Arguments for Christ?

[1]Michael Maudlin, "1993 Christianity Today Book Awards," *Christianity Today,* April 5, 1993, p. 28.

[2]C. S. Lewis, *Surprised by Joy: The Shape of My Early Life* (New York: Harcourt Brace, 1984), pp. 228-29.

[3]Austin Farrer, "The Christian Apologist," cited in *C. S. Lewis at the Breakfast Table and Other Reminiscences,* ed. James T. Como (New York: Harcourt Brace, 1992), p. 142.

[4]Interview with Kenneth Tynan, cited in *In Search of C. S. Lewis,* ed. Stephen Schonfield (South Plainfield, N.J.: Bridge: 1983), pp. 6-7.

[5]From a letter to the editor of *The Canadian C. S. Lewis Journal,* cited in *In Search of C. S. Lewis,* ed. Stephen Schonfield (South Plainfield, N.J.: Bridge, 1983), pp. 163-64.

[6]From a conversation with Douglas Gresham at his home in Ireland in June 2001.

[7]Jim Houston, cited in *We Remember C. S. Lewis: Essays and Memoirs,* ed. David Graham (Nashville: Broadman & Holman, 2001), p. 141.

[8]Stuart Barton Babbage, cited in Carolyn Keele, *C. S. Lewis: Speaker and Teacher* (Grand Rapids: Zondervan, 1971), p. 102.

[10]C. S. Lewis, "Is Theology Poetry?" in *The Weight of Glory and Other Addresses* (New York: Touchstone, 1996), p. 106.

Chapter Two: What Were Lewis's Obstacles to Faith?

[1]C. S. Lewis, *Surprised by Joy* (New York: Harcourt Brace, 1984), p. 21.

[2]C. S. Lewis, *Letters of C. S. Lewis,* ed. Walter Hooper, rev. ed. (New York: Harcourt Brace, 1988), p. 24

[3]Lewis, *Surprised by Joy,* p. 62.

[4]Ibid., p. 70.

[5]Ibid., pp. 207-8.

[6]Ibid., p. 65.

[7]Ibid., pp. 134-35.

[8]Ibid., p. 148.

[9]Ibid., p. 135.

[10]Ibid., p. 181.

[11]Ibid., pp. 223-24.

[12]Ibid., pp. 2?8

Chapter Three: Chronological Snobbery

[1]C. S. Lewis, *Surprised by Joy* (New York: Harcourt Brace, 1984), pp. 207-8.

[2]Ibid., p. 207.

[3]C. S. Lewis, *Voyage of the Dawn Treader* (New York: HarperCollins, 1980), pp. 61-62.

[4]C. S. Lewis, "On the Reading of Old Books," in *First and Second Things: Essays on Theology and Ethics,* ed. Walter Hooper (Glasgow: Collins, 1985), pp. 27-28.

[5]G. K. Chesterton, *As I Was Saying: A Chesterton Reader,* ed. Robert Knille (Grand Rapids: Eerdmans, 1985), p. 267.

[6]C. S. Lewis, *Mere Christianity* (New York: Touchstone, 1996), pp. 36-37.

[7]C. S. Lewis, "On the Transmission of Christianity," in *First and Second Things,* ed. Walter Hooper (Glasgow: Collins, 1985), p. 64.

[8]Ibid., p. 65.

[9]Ibid.

[10]C. S. Lewis, "De Descriptione Temporum," in *Selected Literary Essays* (Cambridge: Cambridge University Press, 1969), p. 13.

[11]Ibid., p. 13.

[12]Ibid., p. 14.

[13]Ibid., p. 11.

[14]See Thomas C. Oden's systematic theology, particularly volume 1, *The Living God* (San Francisco: Harper & Row, 1987), p. 13.

[15]Thomas C. Oden, *After Modernity—What?* (Grand Rapids: Zondervan, 1992), p. 22.

[16]C. S. Lewis, "Membership," in *The Weight of Glory and Other Addresses* (New York: Touchstone, 1996), p. 131.

[17]C. S. Lewis, *Experiment in Criticism* (Cambridge: Cambridge University Press, 1961), pp. 105-6.

[18]C. S. Lewis, *The Four Loves* (New York: Harcourt Brace, 1960), p. 188.

[19]Lewis, *Mere Christianity,* p. 60.

Chapter Four: The Problem of Evil

[1]C. S. Lewis, *The Problem of Pain* (New York: Macmillan, 1969), pp. 104-5.

[2]C. S. Lewis, *Miracles* (New York: Macmillan, 1947), p. 132.

[3]Alvin Plantinga, *God, Freedom and Evil* (Grand Rapids: Eerdmans, 1974), p. 26. In my restatement I have changed Plantinga's language to be more accessible to the average reader. His exact language goes like this:

(1) An omnipotent, omniscient, omnibenevolent God created the world.

(2) God creates a world containing evil and has a good reason for doing so.

(3) Therefore, the world contains evil.

If premise (2) is logically possible, then this set of ideas is not necessarily inconsistent. Thus this set of ideas is demonstrated to be consistent.

[4]For a further discussion of this approach, see Ronald Nash, *Faith and Reason* (Grand Rapids: Zondervan, 1988), pp. 177-94.

[5]C. S. Lewis, *Problem of Pain,* p. 55.

[6]Norman Geisler, *Roots of Evil* (Grand Rapids: Zondervan, 1978), p. 45. Norman Geisler of Southern Evangelical Seminary has argued that God's way is the best of all possible ways to the best of all possible worlds.

[7]Lewis, *Problem of Pain,* p. 30.

[8]Ibid., p. 33.

[9]F. R. Tennant, *Philosophical Theology* (New York: Cambridge University Press, 1928), 2:199-200.

[10]Lewis, *Problem of Pain,* p. 32.

[11]C. S. Lewis, *The Screwtape Letters* (New York: Macmillan, 1961), pp. 101-2.

[12]Lewis, *Problem of Pain,* p. 108.

[13]Ibid., pp. 93-95.

[14]Ibid., p. 96.

[15]C. S. Lewis, ed., *Essays Presented to Charles Williams* (Grand Rapids: Eerdmans, 1966), p. xiii.

[16]Lewis, *Problem of Pain,* pp. 9-10.

[17]Joy Gresham Lewis, from an afterword by Chad Walsh in C. S. Lewis, *A Grief Observed* (New York: Bantam Books, 1976), p. 141.

[18]C. S. Lewis, *A Grief Observed* (New York: Bantam Books, 1976), p. 147.

[19]Ibid., p. 4.

[20]Ibid., p. 5.

[21]Ibid., pp. 45-46.

[22]Ibid., pp. 47-48.

[23]Ibid., p. 51.

[24]Ibid., pp. 53-54.

[25]Ibid., p. 71.

[26]Ibid., pp. 80-81.

[27]Ibid., p. 10,

Chapter Five: Myth

[1]C. S. Lewis, *Miracles* (New York: Macmillan, 1947), p. 139 n. 1.

[2]C. S. Lewis, *Surprised by Joy* (New York: Harcourt Brace, 1984), pp. 62-63.

[3]Ibid., p. 73.

[4]C. S. Lewis, *Letters of C. S. Lewis* (New York: Harcourt Brace, 1988), p. 52.

[5]Ibid.

[6]Lewis, *Surprised by Joy,* p. 69.

[7]C. S. Lewis, *All My Road Before Me: The Diary of C. S. Lewis 1922-1927,* ed. Walter Hooper (New York: Harcourt Brace, 1991), p. 393.

[8]J. R. R. Tolkien, letter 31 in *The Letters of J. R. R. Tolkien,* ed. Humphrey Carpenter (New York: Houghton Mifflin, 1981), p. 147.

[9]J. R. R. Tolkien, "On Fairy Stories," in *The Monsters and the Critics and Other Essays* (London: George Allen & Unwin, 1984), pp. 153-54.

[10]Ibid., pp. 156-57.

[11]Lewis, *Surprised by Joy,* p. 236.

[12]Lewis, *Letters of C. S. Lewis,* p. 288.

[13]Lewis, *Miracles,* p. 117.

[14]C. S. Lewis, "Modern Theology and Biblical Criticism," in *Christian Reflections* (Grand Rapids: Eerdmans, 1967), p. 152.

[15]Ibid., p. 155.

[16]Ibid., p. 156.

[17]Ibid., p. 157.

[18]Ibid.

[19]This information is taken from a videotape of Dr. Kenneth Bailey giving a talk at the Church of the Ascension in Pittsburgh titled "The Reliability of the Oral Tradition Behind the Synoptic Gospels," January 20, 2002. See also the written article "Informal Controlled Oral Tradition and the Synoptic Gospels," *Asia Journal of Theology* 5, no. 1, pp. 34-54.

[20]Ibid.

[21]Helpful books arguing against the critical approach to Scripture include Luke Timothy Johnson, *The Real Jesus* (San Francisco: HarperCollins, 1996), and Michael J. Wilkins and J. P. Moreland, *Jesus Under Fire* (Grand Rapids: Zondervan, 1995).

[22]Lewis, "Modern Theology and Biblical Criticism," p. 158.

[23]For further development of this theme, read Thomas Oden's *After Modernity—What?* a critique by a former liberal critic of the broken promises of the critical method.

[24]Lewis, "Modern Theology and Biblical Criticism," p. 160.

[25]Ibid.

[26]Ibid.

[27]C. S. Lewis, *Letters to Malcolm* (New York: Harcourt Brace, 1964), p. 119.

[28]Lewis, "Modern Theology and Biblical Criticism," p. 166.

Chapter Six: Rationalism

[1]C. S. Lewis, *Mere Christianity* (New York: Touchstone, 1996), p. 124.

[2]C. S. Lewis, *The Pilgrim's Regress* (Grand Rapids: Eerdmans, p. 1989), p. 35.

[3]Ibid.

[4]Ibid., pp. 37-38.

[5]See, for instance, Ronald Nash, *The Concept of God* (Grand Rapids: Zondervan, 1983); Richard Swinburne, *The Coherence of Theism* (Oxford: Clarendon, 1977); and Alvin Plantinga, *God, Freedom and Evil* (New York: Macmillan, 1968).

[6]Lewis, *Mere Christianity,* pp. 124-25.

[7]C. S. Lewis, "On Obstinacy in Belief," in *The World's Last Night and Other Essays* (New York: Harcourt Brace, 1959), p. 23.

Chapter Seven: Imagination

[1]C. S. Lewis, *Surprised by Joy* (New York: Harcourt Brace, 1984), p. 181.

[2]Ibid., p. 170.

[3]Ibid., pp. 213-14.

[4]J. R. R. Tolkien, *The Letters of J. R. R. Tolkien,* ed. Humphrey Carpenter (New York: Houghton Mifflin, 2000), p. 172.

[5]C. S. Lewis, "On Juvenile Tastes," in *Of Other Worlds* (New York: Harcourt Brace, 1966), pp. 40-41.

[6]C. S. Lewis, *They Stand Together: The Letters of C. S. Lewis to Arthur Greeves (1914-1963),* ed. Walter Hooper (London: Collins, 1979), p. 474.

[7]C. S. Lewis, "Hamlet: The Prince or the Poem?" in *Selected Literary Essays,* ed. Walter Hooper (Cambridge: Cambridge University Press, 1969), p. 105.

[8]C. S. Lewis, *Experiment in Criticism* (Cambridge: Cambridge University Press, 1961), p. 72.

[9]J. R. R. Tolkien, "On Fairy Stories," in *The Monsters and the Critics and Other Essays,* ed. Christopher Tolkien (London: George Allen & Unwin, 1983), p. 148

[10]James V. Schall, "On the Reality of Fantasy," in *Tolkien: A Celebration,* ed. Joseph Pearce (San Francisco: Ignatius Press, 1999), p. 71.

[11]Steven R. Lawhead, "J. R. R. Tolkien: Master of Middle Earth," in *Tolkien: A Celebration,* ed. Joseph Pearce (San Francisco: Ignatius Press, 1999), pp. 167-68.

[12]Lewis, *Experiment in Criticism,* p. 19.

Chapter Eight: Miracles

[1]C. S. Lewis, *Miracles* (New York: Macmillan, 1960), p. 15.

[2]Ibid., p. 18.

[3]Richard Purtill, *Reason to Believe* (Grand Rapids: Eerdmans, 1974), p. 44.

[4]Basil Mitchell, interviewed by Andrew Walker in *A Christian for All Christians* (Washington, D.C.: Regnery Gateway, 1992), p. 8.

[5]John Beversluis, "Surprised by Freud: A Critical Appraisal of A. N. Wilson's Biography of C. S. Lewis," *Christianity and Literature* 41, no. 2 (1992): 179-95, cited in Victor Reppert, *C. S. Lewis's Dangerous Idea* (Downers Grove, Ill.: InterVarsity Press, 2003), pp. 17-10.

[6]Basil Mitchell, interviewed by Andrew Walker in *A Christian for All Christians,* p. 10.

[7]Reppert, *C. S. Lewis's Dangerous Idea,* pp. 57-58.

[8]C. S. Lewis, *Reflections on the Psalms* (New York: Harcourt Brace, 1958), pp. 109-10.

[9]Lewis, *Miracles,* p. 102.

[10]Ibid., pp. 100-101.

[11]Ibid., p. 132.

[12]Ibid., p. 133.

[13]Reported in Geoffrey Ashe, *Miracles* (London: Routledge & Kegan Paul, 1978), p. 135, cited by David Clark, "Miracles in the World Religions," in *The Defense of Miracles,* ed. R. Douglas Geivett and Gary R. Habermas (Downers Grove, Ill.: InterVarsity Press, 1997), p. 203.

[14]Lewis, *Miracles,* p. 133.

[15]See Clark, in *Defense of Miracles,* pp. 203, 211.

Chapter Nine: Wish Fulfillment

[1]C. S. Lewis, *The Silver Chair* (New York: HarperCollins, 1981), pp. 190-91.

[2]C. S. Lewis, *The Pilgrim's Regress* (Grand Rapids: Eerdmans, 1989), pp. 58-59. The letters *S* and *J* were added to the text.

[3]See B. F. Skinner, *Beyond Freedom and Dignity* (Indianapolis: Hackett, 2002).

[4]C. S. Lewis, *Mere Christianity* (New York: Touchstone, 1996), p. 120.

[5]Ibid.

[6]Ibid., p. 121.

[7]Ibid.

[8]Lewis, *Pilgrim's Regress,* pp. 71-72. The letters R and J were added to the text.

[9]C. S. Lewis, "Bulverism," in *First and Second Things: Essays on Theology and Ethics* (Glasgow: William Collins, 1985), p. 15.

[10]Ibid.

[11]Ibid., p. 16.

[12]Ibid., p. 17.

[13]Lewis, *Pilgrim's Regress,* p. 72.

[14]Lewis, "Bulverism," p. 16.

[15]Paul Johnson, *Intellectuals* (New York: Harper & Row, 1988), pp. 68-69.

[16]Michael Bakunin, cited in ibid., p. 72.

[17]Techow, cited in Johnson, *Intellectuals,* p. 72.

[18]Lewis, "Bulverism," pp. 13-14.

[19]Ibid., p. 17.

Chapter Ten: Postmodernism

[1]C. S. Lewis, "Christianity and Culture," *Christian Reflections,* ed. Walter Hooper (Grand Rapids: Eerdmans, 1967), p. 23.

[2]C. S. Lewis, "Meditation on a Toolshed," in *First and Second Things* (Glasgow: William Collins, 1985), p. 50.

[3]C. S. Lewis, *The Discarded Image* (Cambridge: Cambridge University Press, 1964), pp. 222-26.

[4]C. S. Lewis, "De Descriptione Temporum," in *Selected Literary Essays,* ed. Walter Hooper (Cambridge: Cambridge University Press, 1980), pp. 2-3.

[5]C. S. Lewis, *A Grief Observed* (New York: Bantam Books, 1976), pp. 76, 77.

[6]C. S. Lewis, "On the Reading of Old Books," in *First and Second Things* (Glasgow: William Collins, 1985), pp. 25-33.

[7]Jonathan Culler, cited in David Lehman, *Signs of the Times* (New York: Poseiden, 1991), pp. 61-62.

[8]Millard J. Erickson, *Truth or Consequences* (Downers Grove, Ill.: InterVarsity Press, 2001), p. 209. Erickson quotes Sandra Harding as claiming that relativism is "fundamentally a sexist response that attempts to preserve the legitimacy of androcentric claims in the face of contrary evidence."

[9]C. S. Lewis, "The Poison of Subjectivism," in *Christian Reflections,* ed. Walter Hooper (Grand Rapids: Eerdmans, 1967), p. 77.

[10]Ibid., pp. 77-78.

[11]C. S. Lewis, *An Experiment in Criticism* (Cambridge: Cambridge University Press, 1961), pp. 19, 140.

[12]Ibid., p. 138.

[13]C. S. Lewis, *The Abolition of Man* (New York: Macmillan, 1955), p. 78.

[14]Lewis, *Experiment in Criticism,* pp. 105-6.

Chapter Eleven: Relativism
[1]C. S. Lewis, *Mere Christianity* (New York: Touchstone, 1996), pp. 45-46.

[2]Ibid., p. 17.

[3]Ibid.

[4]C. S. Lewis, *The Abolition of Man* (New York: Macmillan, 1955).

[5]Ibid., p. 14.

[6]Ibid., pp. 16-17.

[7]Ibid., p. 24.

[8]Ibid., p. 35.

[9]Ibid., pp. 40-41.

[10]Ibid., pp. 43-44.

[11]Arthur Allen Leff, "Unspeakable Ethics, Unnatural Law," *Duke Law Journal,* December 1979, p. 1230.

[12]James Hunter, *The Death of Character* (New York: Basic Books, 2000), p. xv.

[13]Benito Mussolini, cited in Peter Kreeft, *A Refutation of Moral Relativism* (San Francisco: Ignatius Press, 1999), p. 18.

[14]James Miller, *The Passion of Michel Foucault* (Cambridge, Mass.: Harvard University Press, 1993), p. 384.

[15]Ibid.

[16]Lewis, *Abolition of Man,* p. 78.

Chapter Twelve: Other Religions
[1]C. S. Lewis, *The Silver Chair* (New York: HarperCollins, 1981), pp. 20-21.

[2]C. S. Lewis, *Mere Christianity* (New York: Touchstone, 1996), p. 43.

[3]C. S. Lewis, *The Problem of Pain* (New York: Macmillan, 1960), pp. 13-25.

[4]Ibid., p. 18.

[5]Ibid., pp. 20-21.

[6]C. S. Lewis, *The Abolition of Man* (New York: Macmillan, 1955), p. 29.

[7]Ibid., p. 84.

[8]Lewis, *Problem of Pain,* p. 23.

[9]C. S. Lewis, *Arthurian Torso: Williams and the Arthuriad* (Oxford: Oxford University Press, 1948), p. 124.

[10]C. S. Lewis, in a letter written December 14, 1950, to Sheldon Vanauken in *A Severe Mercy* (San Francisco: Harper & Row, 1977), p. 90.

[11]C. S. Lewis, "What Are We to Make of Jesus Christ?" in *God in the Dock* (Grand Rapids: Eerdmans, 1970), pp. 157-58.

[12]C. S. Lewis, "Chrsitian Apologetics," in *God in the Dock* (Grand Rapids: Eerdmans, 1970), pp. 102-3.

[13]Ibid.

[14]C. S. Lewis, *Surprised by Joy* (New York: Harcourt Brace, 1984), pp. 235-36.

[15]C. S. Lewis, *Letters of C. S. Lewis,* ed. Walter Hooper, rev. ed. (New York: Harcourt Brace, 1988), p. 453.

[16]See Art Lindsley, *True Truth* (Downers Grove, Ill.: Intervarsity Press, 2004), pp. 169-70.

[17]Lewis, *Mere Christianity,* p. 45.
[18]C. S. Lewis, *The Last Battle* (New York: HarperCollins, 1984), pp. 204-6.
[19]Lewis, *Letters of C. S. Lewis,* p. 428.

Chapter Thirteen: Death and Immortality

[1]C. S. Lewis, "Weight of Glory," in *The Weight of Glory and Other Addresses* (New York: Touchstone, 1996), p. 39.
[2]From the preface by Walter Hooper in C. S. Lewis, *Christian Reflections,* ed. Walter Hooper (Grand Rapids: Eerdmans, 1967), p. xi.
[3]C. S. Lewis, *Mere Christianity* (New York: Touchstone, 1996), p. 87.
[4]C. S. Lewis, *Reflections on the Psalms* (New York: Harcourt Brace, 1958), p. 40.
[5]C. S. Lewis, *English Literature in the Sixteenth Century* (Oxford: Clarendon Press, 1954), p. 188.
[6]C. S. Lewis, *Problem of Pain* (New York: Macmillan, 1969), p. 145.
[7]C. S. Lewis, *The Letters of C. S. Lewis,* ed. Walter Hooper, rev. ed. (New York: Harcourt Brace, 1988), p. 438.
[8]C. S. Lewis, *The Silver Chair* (New York: HarperCollins, 1981), pp. 251-53.
[9]C. S. Lewis, *The Last Battle* (New York: HarperCollins, 1981), p. 228.
[10]C. S. Lewis, *A Grief Observed* (New York: Bantam Books, 1976), p. 83.
[11]W. H. Lewis, "Memoir of C. S. Lewis," in *Letters of C. S. Lewis,* p. 45.
[12]See, for example, Lee Strobel, *The Case for Christ* (Grand Rapids: Zondervan, 1998); William Lane Craig, *The Son Rises* (Chicago: Moody Press, 1981); Gary R. Habermas, *The Resurrection of Jesus* (Grand Rapids: Eerdmans, 1975); George E. Ladd, *I Believe in the Resurrection of Jesus* (Grand Rapids: Eerdmans, 1975); Merrill C. Tenny, *The Reality of the Resurrection* (New York: Harper and Row, 1963).
[13]Lewis, *Mere Christianity,* p. 119.

Chapter Fourteen: Christ

[1]C. S. Lewis, *The Lion, the Witch and the Wardrobe* (New York: HarperCollins, 1978), pp. 74-75.
[2]Ibid., p. 85.
[3]Ibid., p. 86.
[4]C. S. Lewis, *The Horse and His Boy* (New York: HarperCollins, 1982), pp. 175-76.
[5]C. S. Lewis, *The Voyage of the Dawn Treader* (New York: HarperCollins, 1980), pp. 115-16.
[6]Lewis, *Lion, the Witch and the Wardrobe,* p. 155.
[7]Ibid., p. 163.
[8]Ibid., p. 177.
[9]Ibid., pp. 178-79.
[10]C. S. Lewis, *Mere Christianity* (New York: Touchstone, 1996), pp. 55-56.

Index